The FORBIDDEN CITY within Victoria

Merry Christmas 1992
Love from Russ

加拿大最早之唐人街

黎全恩

The Forbidden City within Victoria

David Chuenyan Lai

Orca Book Publishers

First Edition

Canadian Cataloguing in Publication Data
Lai, Chuen-yan David, 1937-
The forbidden city within Victoria

Includes biblioigraphical references and index.
ISBN 0-920501-63-X

1. Chinatown (Victoria, B.C.) — History. 2. Chinese — British Columbia — Victoria — History. 3. Chinese Canadians — British Columbia — Victoria — History.* I. Title.
FC3846.p.C5L34 1991 971.1'28004951 F1089.5.V6L34 1991
C991-091539-3

Financially assisted by the Canada Council and by the Ministry of Municipal Affairs, Recreation and Culture through the British Columbia Heritage Trust.

Cover Design: Susan Fergusson
Printed and bound in Canada

Orca Book Publishers
P.O. Box 5626, Station B
Victoria, B.C., Canada, V8R 6S4

To all the dedicated people who have helped rehabilitate and preserve the earliest Chinatown in Canada

Contents

List of Figures

List of Tables

Photo Credits

All photos property of the author except:

City of Victoria: #11, 18, 36, 53, 57, 82, 83, 87, 88, 95, 99, 100, 103
Jim Ryan: #8
National Archives of Canada: #2
Provincial Archives of British Columbia: #94, 96, 97
Times Colonist: #9
Yim Leong: #5, 50, 64, 84, 92, 93, 98

Preface

Chinatown! Some people instantly conjure a place with an aura of mystery: underground tunnels, secret gambling dens, and hidden opium rooms. These elements, which have created much of the mystique associated with Chinatown, have long vanished or were never in existence, but memories of them are still very much alive among some people. Intricate networks of narrow passageways and claustrophobic courtyards were and are still found behind the commercial facades of old buildings in Victoria's Chinatown. For a long time, many Western people were unfamiliar with this inner-city neighbourhood, conceiving it as a godforsaken enclave of vices, a "forbidden town" that no decent white people would dare enter. Even today, Victoria's Chinatown still seems set apart by differences in language, customs, and streetscape.

It is my contention that in trying to understand Victoria's Chinatown today, we need to know about its past, and the impact of traditional Chinese culture on it. Most Chinatown myths are invented stories that play on the imagination of tourists and are passed on. This book attempts to contrast Chinatown's myths with its realities. By dispelling the myths, I do not intend to destroy visitors' curiosity about Chinatown. Instead, I wish to make Chinatown a little more intelligible to them, thereby enhancing their interest and appreciation of its physical and cultural heritage. Although buildings in Chinatown are constructed in Western styles, their distinctive architectural features, such as curved roofs and upturned eaves, display the Chinese influence and create a unique streetscape. Why are Chinatown's buildings usually decorated with tiled roofs and upturned eaves? What do the terra cotta animals on the Chinatown Gate represent? Are there underground passages in Chinatown? Where do the narrow alleys lead? How was Fan Tan Alley created? Are gambling dens still being run secretly in Chinatown? Who is the God of Tam Kung? What are "tongs"? Why are the roofs of Chinese buildings curved upward? What is the origin of Chinese gates? The list of queries about Victoria's Chinatown is endless. This book attempts to answer these and other related questions, providing readers with a better understanding of the history, symbolism, architectural features, and streetscape of Victoria's Chinatown.

The book consists of fourteen chapters. Chapter 1 relates the growth of Victoria's Chinatown from 1858 to 1991. Chapter 2 traces the 134-year history of Chinese ownership of properties in Chinatown. Chapter 3 describes the origins of some peculiar surnames of Chinese in Victoria. Chapters 4 through 7 contrast the myths with the realities of Chinatown's tunnels, alleys, temples, and gambling games. Chapters 8 and 9 deal with the symbolism of the gateway, sidewalks, and decorative components of building facades. Chapters 10 through 13 include photographs of thirty-two heritage buildings in Chinatown, and describe their ownership patterns and historical and architectural importance. The final chapter gives a self-guided walking tour of the "forbidden town," making use of old photographs to compare its past with its present streetscape.

There are many variations in the transliteration of Chinese names because of different dialects. This book uses the well-established or more familiar spellings for place names, personal names, and names of stores and voluntary associations, because many readers may find the Pinyin system spellings difficult to recognize. Hence, Hong Kong, Tam Kung, and Dart Coon Club are retained in preference to Xianggang, Tan Gong, and Daquanshe. However, the Pinyin system of romanization is used for spellings of places, persons, and associations if they do not have conventional English names.

I would like to thank the staff of the Provincial Archives of British Columbia and the City of Victoria Archives for their assistance with access to reference materials; Clem Finney, Robert Tyrrell and Vivian Sinclair for editing the manuscript; Miss Joan Man Lai for proofreading; Messrs. Ole Heggen and Ken Josephson for preparing illustrations and doing cartographic work; Mr. Windsor Chan, Mr. Raymond Candy, Mr. David Craig, and Miss Tanya Friese for assistance in library research and field surveys; Mr. Rick Sykes for installing the computer programs; and Ms. Judy Simpson and Ms. Ruth Steinfatt for printing the manuscript. I wish to express special thanks to Dr. Anthony Yeh, acting assistant director of the Centre of Urban Planning and Environmental Management, University of Hong Kong, for permission to use the Centre's research facilities while I was carrying out my research on this book during my study leave in the spring of 1991. Thanks also go to many interviewees who contributed information on the history of Chinese people and Chinatown in Victoria. I am grateful to the Secretary of State, Department of Multiculturalism, for awarding me two grants for the Chinatown researches; this volume is partly based on these two research projects. I also wish to thank the University of Victoria for supporting the research for this book with a study leave grant in lieu of salary.

David Chuenyan Lai
Victoria, 1991

« 1 » Growth of Victoria's Chinatown, 1858 – 1991

For nearly a century, Victoria's Chinatown captured the imagination of many Western people. To them, it was an enclave of vices, a "Forbidden Town" that opened only to the Chinese; any decent white person would stay away from this mysterious labyrinth. The Chinese, however, considered it their home, where they could follow their customs, speak their dialects, and find pleasure, comfort, and companionship. Largely ostracized from Canadian society, they did not feel safe and secure once they were outside Chinatown; its Forbidden Town reputation insulated them from the hostility of the white public. In this book, I consider Chinatown as a multifaceted built environment, describe it as a cultural and social entity, and examine its socioeconomic functions and visual elements. Thus, many old and current photographs, maps, and diagrams are used to display and interpret its history, symbolism, structural interiors, building facades, and urban scenes. I have also carried out field surveys in Hong Kong and Guangzhou to study the influence of Chinese culture on the streetscape of Chinatown.

The First Arrivals

The migration of Chinese to Canada began in 1858, when gold was discovered in the lower Fraser River in British Columbia. Chinese living in San Francisco were the first to hear of these strikes. On 15 May 1858, *The Daily Globe*, a San Francisco newspaper, reported that

> *a very intelligent Chinaman, named Ah Hong, who has lived in Marysville a long time, has just returned from a visit to the Fraser River Gold Region, where he was sent, as an explorer, by some of his Mongolian countrymen of San Francisco. Ah Hong's account of the marvellous richness of the gold mines of that region is perfectly bewildering. He represents the miners as taking out the precious metal by the bucketful.... A great number of Chinese, moved by his representations, are preparing to migrate to the North.*[1]

A month later, *The Victoria Gazette*, a newspaper of the City of Victoria, the Colony of Vancouver Island, carried a report that "a batch of celestials have landed from the *Oregon*, (camping) in the vicinity of a sign which bears the euphonious and suggestive legend, Chang Tsoo. Doubtless ere long the familiar interrogation of 'Wantee Washee?' will be added to our every day conversational vocabulary."[2] Hence, the first group of Chinese emigrants to Canada must have landed in Victoria in June 1858.

Initially, all Chinese immigrants came to Victoria by boat from San Francisco. Soon other Chinese came directly from China, landing at Victoria to obtain mining licences and prepare their packs before heading off to the mainland. An old-timer recalled the scene of the Chinese arrival in Victoria:

> *The first large load of Chinese upon landing here presented a rare sight. Crowds of these men were huddled together in a sailing vessel, chatting and motioning to one another in a strange manner. Each had a bundle under his arm or on his back, his only possessions. Others had two bundles on a carrying-stick across their shoulders. Their hair was done up in queues; some had it hanging in long braids down their backs. Dressed in an unusual style, with trouser legs a foot or more wide, their overblouse (usually dark blue) had wide sleeves. The sight was both*

novel and interesting. There was an entire absence of women.[3]

Most of the Chinese arrivals, like other gold-seekers, took the first available boats to the Fraser River, but a few merchants, artisans, and craftsmen stayed behind to set up stores on Cormorant Street between Douglas and Government streets, where the embryo of Canada's first Chinatown was formed. Its growth can be described according to the Old Chinatown Development Model outlined in my book *Chinatowns: Towns Within Cities in Canada*.[4] The model describes the development of an Old Chinatown in four stages: budding, blooming, withering, and reviving. Each stage, with its own demographic, socioeconomic, and physical characteristics, has been shaped by immigration policies, attitudes of the host society, urban renewal programs, the economic condition of the city and the province, and other factors.

The Budding Period, 1858-1870s

A few Chinese merchants from San Francisco bought properties in Victoria soon after they arrived in the summer of 1858. Loo Chuck Fan and Chang Tsoo, for example, bought properties on Cormorant Street, where they set up wooden huts in preparation for their recruited labourers from China (Fig. 1). Western property owners also built wooden shacks on the same street and leased them to other Chinese arrivals. The budding Chinatown on Cormorant Street, separated from the city centre by the Johnson Street ravine, was accessible from the south only via three narrow footbridges, which spanned the ravine at Store, Government, and Douglas streets (Fig. 2).

When the City of Victoria was incorporated in 1862, about three hundred people – or six percent of its population – were Chinese. Virtually all of them were young males who resided in Chinatown. Most of them were employed by the few large Chinese companies, such as Kwong Lee & Co., Tai Soong & Co., and Yang Wo Sang & Co. Headquartered in San Francisco, these companies set up branches in Victoria, Hope, Yale, and other gold-mining towns, and arranged for Chinese labourers to come to British Columbia.

During the 1870s, a class of small merchants began to emerge in Victoria's Chinatown, which was characterized by a

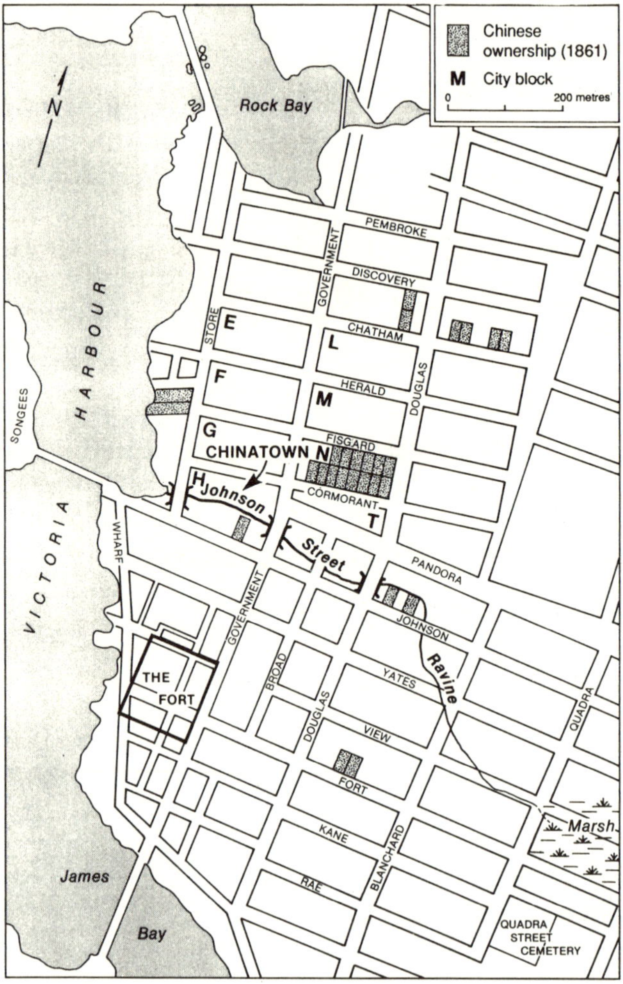

Fig. 1. Location of Victoria's Chinatown, 1861.

linear commercial development along a single street. Small grocery stores, butcher's shops, and other small Chinese business concerns were concentrated on Cormorant Street. On Government Street near Chinatown, a Chinese mission school was opened in 1874 by the Methodist Church, and a Chinese temple was established two years later by the Hakka natives.

The Blooming Period, 1880s-1910s

The national census of 1881, which included British Columbia for the first time, listed 693 Chinese in Victoria.[5] This head count

Fig. 2. A footbridge spanning Johnson Street ravine at Government Street, 1879.

made Victoria's Chinatown the largest Chinese settlement in Canada. But that was just the beginning. Between 1881 and 1884, nearly sixteen thousand Chinese arrived in Victoria, from China, San Francisco, and Puget Sound ports.[6] Thousands of them soon left for the mainland to help build the British Columbia section of the Canadian Pacific Railway. Since Victoria was the gateway to Canada from China, its Chinatown prospered. By 1886 it covered an area of more than four city blocks north of the Johnson Street ravine, and housed eighty-seven percent of Victoria's 2,988 Chinese (Table 1, pg. 15). At that time, the city of Vancouver did not yet exist, and its predecessor, the town of Granville, had only three Chinese stores and fewer than fifty Chinese residents.

Victoria experienced a major building boom between the 1890s and the 1910s, during which many wooden frame houses in Chinatown were replaced by three-storey brick buildings. These new structures displayed recessed balconies on front facades and other features commonly associated with Chinatown buildings. The sidewalks were covered with planks and sheltered by simple wooden verandas (see Fig. 53 and Fig. 96). Behind the commercial facades of the buildings was a

Fig. 3. An interior courtyard.

maze of claustrophobic courtyards, picturesque arcades, and narrow alleys (see Fig. 4). These interconnecting passageways, closed off from public view, led to tenements, opium dens, gambling clubs, and other socioeconomic activities. Interior courtyards, which served to provide open spaces, light, and ventilation, were entered through gaps between small lanes, or through narrow corridors of tenement buildings (Fig. 3). Outsiders could not find their way out once they entered Chinatown; its streetscape or lanescape was similar to an ancient Chinese town with a maze of alleys and narrow lanes.

Chinatown had reached its apogee in the early 1910s, covering about six city blocks and housing most of the city's three thousand Chinese (Fig. 4). The Esquimalt and Nanaimo Railway terminated on Store Street, and the Victoria and Sidney Railway on Fisgard Street; the area surrounding Chinatown abounded with western hotels and saloons. The headquarters of all of the Chinese clan, county, and other associations in Canada were established in Victoria's Chinatown. Most of the Chinese import and export companies, retail stores, and other business concerns were located there as well. In its prime, Chinatown boasted more than 150 firms, two theatres, a hospital, three Chinese schools, two churches, more than five temples or

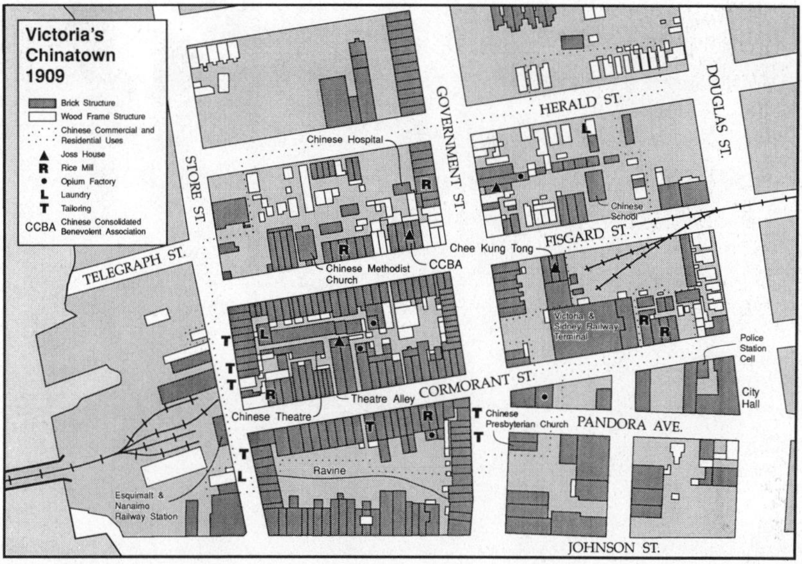

Fig. 4. Victoria's Chinatown, 1909.

shrines, and over ten opium factories, and many gambling dens, and brothels. Most of the Chinatown buildings served several purposes. The Chinese Consolidated Benevolent Association building, for example, trebled as a school, a temple, and a public meeting place. A merchant, with his wares in front, lived with his family in the rooms upstairs or at the rear. A herbalist shop might sell Chinese herbs as well as groceries, and engage in tailoring (Fig. 5). The mixture of commercial, residential, industrial, educational, and recreational uses, and the Oriental decorative facades of buildings, gave Chinatown a unique townscape, obviously distinguished from other parts of the city.

Chinatown, then, was a fully self-contained community and a headquarters of the Chinese in Canada; it functioned as a training base where new arrivals were exposed to Western culture, taught to master English, and trained to survive in Canadian society. Those who learned the ropes and acquired a trade often moved on to other parts of Victoria or to other cities to begin new lives. When unemployed and poor, they fell back on Chinatown for help.

The Chinese population in Victoria increased steadily, from 2,080 in 1891 to 2,978 in 1901 and to 3,458 in 1911, and was still predominated by single males. In 1911, for example, the sex ratio was nearly 1,300 males to 100 females. Thus, the Chinese society in

Fig. 5. A store at 555 Fisgard Street in the 1920s, selling Chinese herbs, dry goods and grocery products.

the city was still a "bachelor" society. Only a few wealthy merchants had comfortable family lives; the great majority of the Chinese led a lonely and difficult existence in Canada.

The Withering Period, 1920s–1970s

After the turn of the twentieth century, Victoria's Chinatown was outstripped by Vancouver's in both population and importance. Having a deeper harbour and being the western terminal of the Canadian Pacific Railway, Vancouver took over trade that had formerly passed through Victoria, gradually replacing Victoria as the premier port on the Pacific coast of Canada. The 1911 national census listed 3,559 Chinese in Vancouver and 3,458 in Victoria; this made Victoria the second largest Chinese settlement in Canada. Another factor that hastened the demographic and economic decline of Victoria's Chinatown was the Chinese Immigration Act of 1923, by which Chinese were virtually prohibited from entering the country.[7] Victoria's Chinese population has been on the decline ever since; it dropped from 3,702 in 1931, to 3,037 in 1941, and to 1,901 in 1951. Deaths, departures for China, and moves to better residential neighbourhoods were three major factors in the depopulation of

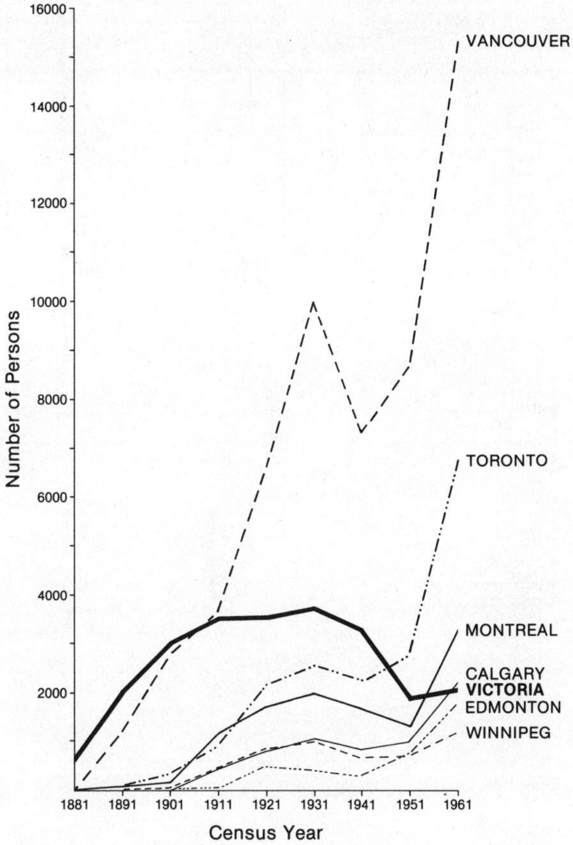

Fig. 6. Chinese Population Growth in Selected Cities, 1881 – 1961.

Chinatown. Nevertheless, Victoria's Chinatown remained the second largest in Canada until the late 1940s, when it was superseded by Toronto's Chinatown (Fig. 6). The labyrinthine characteristic of the Forbidden Town did not change much even in the late 1950s.

Chinese immigration resumed after the Chinese Immigration Act of 1923 was repealed in 1947.[8] Although the Chinese population in Victoria began to increase, by 1961 it had risen to only sixty percent of the record high in 1931. As prejudice and discrimination against Chinese subsided, allowing them to be more easily assimilated into Canadian society, more and more Chinese left Chinatown to seek better accommodation in other parts of the city. Furthermore, under the non-discriminatory

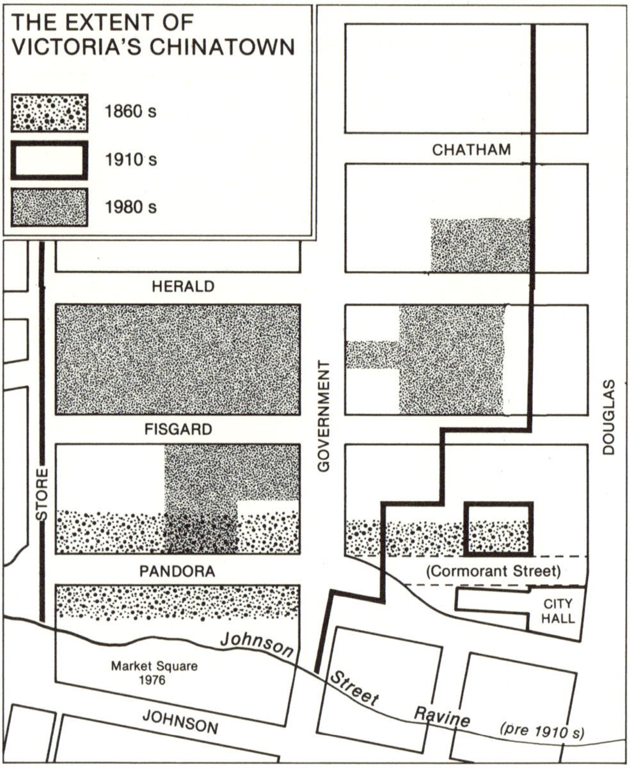

Fig. 7. The areal extent of Chinatown, 1860s – 1980s.

immigration policy of 1967, Chinese immigrants, like immigrants of other nationalities, were chosen according to a "points system" based on educational training, occupational skill, knowledge of English and French, and other criteria. Many of these new immigrants were "*Chi-yuppies,*" or Chinese young upwardly mobile professional people. They settled down in Gordon Head and other better residential areas, and turned their backs on Chinatown, which was then in a terribly rundown state. However, Chinatown was still attractive and essential to the "*Chi-eppies,*" or Chinese elderly poor people, many of whom still could not speak English. Clinging to their cultural traditions in Chinatown, they could live in continuity and harmony with the past. Chinatown was equally essential to the "*Chi-lippies,*" or Chinese low-income people. These included many recent immigrants from China and refugees of Chinese ethnic origin from Indochina. Being unable to speak English, they had to use

Chinatown as a transitional place in which they could learn about Canadian culture and adjust to the new environment. Hence, Chinatown was and still is used by many new immigrants as a springboard for acculturation and assimilation into Canadian society.

Throughout the 1960s and early 1970s, both the area and population of Victoria's Chinatown continued to decrease (Fig. 7). A 1971 field survey of Chinatown revealed that its areal extent had dwindled to about two city blocks, and its residents had decreased to 143.[9] Many dilapidated tenement buildings were condemned, their upper floors boarded up and left vacant. Some old buildings were demolished, and the space converted to parking lots. Chinatown became a blighted neighbourhood, conceived by many local people as an undesirable slum and an eyesore.

Although Chinese immigrants came to Canada in increasing numbers throughout the late 1970s and early 1980s, most of them went to large cities such as Vancouver, Toronto, and Montreal. By 1986, Victoria had dropped to eighth position in Canada in terms of its Chinese population (Table 2, pg. 16).

The Reviving Period, 1980s

Having languished for more than three decades, Victoria's Chinatown seemed to be doomed to extinction, like other Old Chinatowns in Canada. It was eventually saved by City Councils during the mayoralties of Michael Young and Bill Tindall. Alderman Bob Wright, who perceived the economic potential and heritage value of Chinatown, was the driving force behind the launch of a rehabilitation program in July 1979. The program included several projects: painting or cleaning old buildings, installing Chinese-style lamp posts and bilingual street signs, improving sidewalks, planting cherry and pine trees, constructing a Chinatown Care Facility, and erecting a Chinese decorative arch called the Gate of Harmonious Interest.[10] Councils continued the rehabilitation of Chinatown during the mayoralties of Peter Pollen and Gretchen Brewin. Fan Tan Alley was refurbished, dilapidated heritage buildings were renovated, and directional signs to the revitalized Chinatown were installed throughout downtown Victoria. The Chung Wah Mansion, a housing project subsidized by the federal government, was built to provide accommodation for Chinese and non-Chinese people with moderate incomes. By

Fig. 8. A visit to Chinatown by Queen Elizabeth II and the Duke of Edinburgh, 8 March 1983.

1991, the number of residents in Chinatown had increased to about three hundred, of which approximately one-third were of Chinese ethnic origin, and there were nearly one hundred business concerns.

Summary

The public image of an Old Chinatown has changed. A rehabilitated Chinatown is no longer perceived as a Forbidden Town; it is considered an integral part of a city's downtown centre, a historic district of rich heritage, and a root of Chinese culture. It is also a mecca for tourists, and is seen as an asset to a city, not a liability. The once rundown Chinatown in Victoria is an excellent example.

This historic area, more than a century old, is a role model for the growth, decline, and revival of Old Chinatowns in North America. Although it has a small Chinese population today, and has lost much of its former lustre and mystery, the remaining

Fig. 9.
On 16 March 1989 Dr. David Lam gave his first throne speech for the Third Session of the Twenty-fourth Parliament of British Columbia.

fragment still possesses its nineteenth-century townscape. It is one of the very few Chinatowns in North America to retain cohesive groupings of old buildings with high heritage values. The labyrinthine features behind them still remain, defining the special heritage character of the once Forbidden Town. A growing consciousness of its heritage among town planners and politicians is now leading to attempts to preserve the fragments of the nineteenth-century landscape of Chinatown and make it a live museum piece or a tourist attraction. In the past few years, Victoria's Chinatown has several times been a location for television and motion picture production. In May 1989, for example, distinguished British filmmaker John Badham used Victoria and its Chinatown in *Bird on a Wire*, a big-budget romantic/adventure film starring Mel Gibson and Goldie Hawn. Recent influxes of tourists and curious visitors to Chinatown reflect its growing economic and historic significance to the City of Victoria.

This tiny Chinese enclave is outstanding in the history of Canadian Chinatowns because it is the first and the oldest surviving Chinatown in Canada. It was the largest Chinatown in Canada for fifty years (1858–1910), and the second largest for forty years (1911–1950). Furthermore, it is the only Canadian

Chinatown that has a complete history, dating from the first Chinese arrival in Canada to the present – a history of 134 years. For nearly three decades before the Canadian Pacific Railway was completed, Victoria was the first port of entry of most Chinese immigrants. Many of their descendants must come to its Chinatown to trace their roots.

Victoria's Chinatown was also the first Canadian Chinatown to carry out a comprehensive rehabilitation program. It was the first to have a permanent Chinese arch, and its Chinese-style street lamp posts were later copied and installed in Chinatowns in Edmonton and Winnipeg. On 8 March 1983, Her Majesty the Queen and His Royal Highness the Duke of Edinburgh visited Victoria and included Chinatown in their tour; no other Canadian Chinatown had been visited by a British monarch before[11] (Fig. 8). Victoria's Chinatown is also the first in Canada to host walking tours by two Lieutenant-Governors. On 18 February 1986, Lieutenant-Governor Robert G. Rogers and Mrs. Rogers visited the Chinese Public School, Tam Kung Temple, and other places of attraction in Chinatown[12]. On 12 February 1989, it was honoured again by the tour of Lieutenant-Governor Dr. David See-Chai Lam and Mrs. Dorothy Lam; Dr. Lam is the first Chinese-Canadian Lieutenant-Governor in Canada[13] (Fig. 9). Such visits have further enhanced the historic significance of the Forbidden Town.

Table 1
Distribution of Chinese in Victoria, April 1886

Location	*No. of Persons*		
	Male	*Female*	*Total*
Chinatown:			
Cormorant St.	1,374	61	1,435
Fisgard St.	449	107	556
Government St.	351	22	373
Store St.	209	10	219
Outside Chinatown:			
Johnson St.	60	–	60
Pandora Ave	51	–	51
Yates St.	61	2	63
Douglas St.	30	2	32
View St.	12	–	12
Blanshard St	11	–	11
Fort St.	6	–	6
Other streets	159	11	170
Total	***2,773***	***215***	***2,988****

Source: Census of Chinese taken by the Police Department, City of Victoria, 1 April 1886.

**This included eighty-six children under 14 years of age.*

Table 2
Chinese Population in Canada, 1986

Metropolitan Areas	*Persons*	
	Number	*% of Total*
Toronto	143,235	34.59
Vancouver	109,370	26.41
Calgary	26,175	6.32
Edmonton	24,560	5.93
Montreal	24,185	5.84
Ottawa-Hull	11,575	2.80
Winnipeg	9,300	2.25
Victoria	**6,295**	**1.52**
Hamilton	4,665	1.13
Saskatoon	3,245	0.78
Regina	2,595	0.63
Kitchener	2,545	0.61
London	2,430	0.59
Windsor	2,390	0.58
St. Catharines-Niagara	1,740	0.42
Oshawa	1,400	0.34
Halifax	1,250	0.30
Quebec City	895	0.22
Thunder Bay	755	0.18
St. John's	690	0.17
Sudbury	505	0.12
Other cities	34,240	8.27
Total	***414,040***	***100.00***

Source: Census of Canada, 1986

«2» *Chinese Ownership of Properties, 1858 - 1991*

> *The first Chinese settlement here (in Victoria) in 1860 was in the Yates, Fort, Quadra, Cook rectangle. It was from a residential point of view a most undesirable area. There was a two-acre lake between Yates and Cook Streets... They (the Chinese) lived there probably not out of choice but of necessity. In the gold rush days all dry land was at a premium and the Chinese were not in a position to pay a premium. Gradually they consolidated their settlement around Government, Fisgard and Herald Streets.*[1]

Many people assumed that the early Chinese immigrants in Victoria were all so poor that they could afford to live only on the undesirable border of the city, where rents were cheaper. This assumption was partially correct; a large proportion of the Chinese immigrants were indeed extremely poor. There were a few rich Chinese merchants, however, whose wealth was at least equal to that of some well-to-do English families in Victoria. Contrary to the popular myth of Chinese poverty, a few Chinese merchants from San Francisco participated in real estate speculation soon after they arrived in Victoria. On 12 July 1858, for example, seven out of seventeen successful bidders at a land auction were Chinese. They bid against others by offering high prices for the seven 30' x 100' lots on Esquimalt Harbour (Table 3, pg. 24). Most of the lots knocked down to the Chinese were purchased later by Ah Sou, a well-known Chinese merchant of San Francisco.[2] The myth that the Chinese could not afford to buy properties in the town centre is also debunked by the 1861 Victoria District Assessment Roll. That year, at least twenty-four lots, valued at $3,012, belonged to the Chinese, and five of them were located south of the Johnson Street ravine[3] (see Fig. 1).

Chinese ownership of properties in Chinatown is studied in this chapter in order to understand the economic power of the Chinese merchants and the degree of their control over the physical and economic characteristics of Chinatown in the past century. The ownership patterns can be chronologically divided into four phases of development: (1) Monopoly of San Francisco Merchants, 1858–1880s, (2) Individual and Institutional Ownership, 1890s–1910s, (3) The Decline in Ownership, 1920s–1930s, and (4) Repossession of Properties, 1940s–1960s.

Monopoly of San Francisco Merchants, 1858 – 1880s

Soon after their arrival in Victoria, Chinese merchants from San Francisco set up branches of their companies and began participating in land speculation. They included Loo Chuck Fan and his brother Loo Chew Fan, who owned Kwong Lee & Co.; Chang Tsoo, who operated Yang Wo Sang & Co.; and Wong Shui Chiu and Tong Kee, who ran Tai Soong & Co. On 24 July 1858, Chang Tsoo and Loo Chuck Fan purchased thirteen lots, at $100 per lot, in Block N on the northern side of Cormorant Street, dividing the land between themselves[4] (see Fig. 1). Half a year later, Chang Tsoo sold two and a half lots to Kong Hop Tong for $800, making a 200 percent profit.[5] Kong Hop Tong then sold the lots to J. P. Couch for $1,800, more than double his purchase price.[6] The land boom lasted for several years, ending in 1865 when Victoria faced an economic recession. Many speculators lost their properties through tax arrears or failure to repay loans. In June 1867, Chang Tsoo and his partner, Li Hing, defaulted on a $10,000 loan and interest, losing all their properties to George Hills.[7] Tai Soong & Co. and Kwong Lee & Co. managed to survive the slump in real estate, mainly because of strong financial

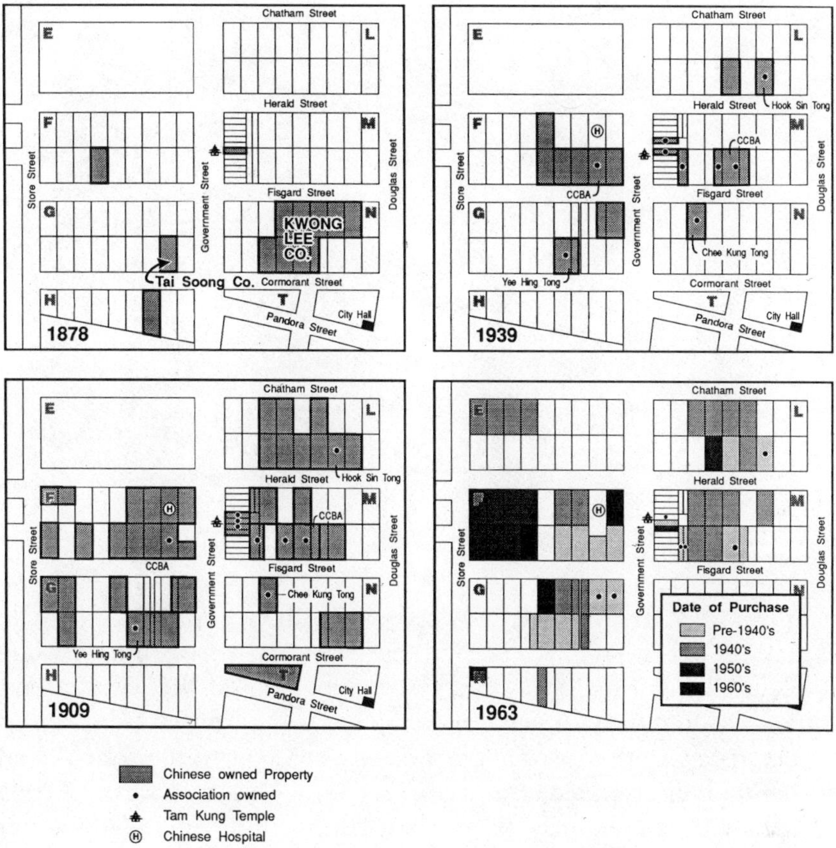

Fig. 10. Patterns of Chinese ownership of properties in Chinatown, 1878 – 1963.

backing from San Francisco. Not only could they hold onto their land, they could also continue to purchase properties. In August 1878, for example, Chun Tan, on behalf of Tai Soong & Co., bought a lot in Block G and moved the company there. It became the first import and export company on that block of Cormorant Street[8] (Fig. 11). Tai Fook Kuan, a gambling club, occupied a portion of the building's ground floor (Fig. 11). In the rear, the Tai Soong Opium Factory operated throughout the 1870s and the 1880s. The other big Chinese landlord in Chinatown was Kwong Lee & Co., which owned eight and a half lots of land in Block N.

Chinatown was busy and prosperous during the early 1880s while the British Columbia section of the Canadian Pacific Railway was being constructed. In 1885 the Chinese

Fig. 11. Tai Soong & Co. at 40 – 42 Cormorant Street (now 550 – 556 Pandora Avenue), 1886.

Consolidated Benevolent Association (CCBA) purchased a lot in Block F of Fisgard Street and erected the first Chinese tong building. This three-storey brick structure housed the association's office, a free school, and a temple. New arrivals from China registered with the association, pupils were sent to the school, and worshippers attended the temple. As a result, Fisgard Street gradually became a busy place, competing with Cormorant Street as the centre of Chinatown.[9] In 1889 the Methodist Church purchased a lot in Block F and erected a church for teaching Chinese children English and preaching their gospel. A year later, the Chinese leased a plot of land in Block G, where they built a large Chinese theatre. In spite of the boom in Chinatown, the Loo family's wealth began to decline. Owing to heavy borrowing and family disputes, the Loo brothers went to court often, eventually going bankrupt. In 1887, all their properties in City Blocks N and H went up for sale by public auction.[10]

Individual and Institutional Ownership, 1890s – 1910s

After the 1890s, a new class of merchants emerged. They were small proprietors who opened restaurants, grocery stores, herb shops, and other businesses in Chinatown. Many family and/or business groups pooled their resources in order to acquire land and premises. In 1909, for example, nearly half of the properties in Chinatown were owned by Chan Tong Ork, Lim Dat, Lee Dye, Lee Mong Kow, Lee Fok Gay, and other Chinese merchants. Not only were they wealthy and influential leaders in the community, they were also spokesmen for the Chinese in Canada before the Chinese Consulate General was established in Ottawa in 1909.

Another significant group of Chinese property owners included county, clan, and other types of voluntary associations. By 1909 ten associations, including Hook Sin Tong, Yee Fung Toy Tong, and the Lee's Association, had their own tong buildings in Chinatown; the CCBA owned four and a half lots in Blocks F and M.

The Decline in Ownership, 1920s – 1930s

Canada experienced a general economic slump after the First World War. Chinese labourers and merchants were again blamed for taking jobs and businesses from the white people, and anti-Chinese sentiments increased. On 28 November 1921, the Victoria Chamber of Commerce recommended to the provincial government that legislation be passed to deny all Orientals future rights to property ownership, and that such persons be debarred from entering Canada.[11] Although no legislative acts were passed to prohibit them from buying properties, the Chinese themselves lost their land through defaulting on mortgage payments and city taxes. The Great Depression of the 1930s accelerated the economic recession in Chinatown. From the late 1910s through the 1930s, thirteen Chinese-owned lots in Chinatown were acquired by the City for tax arrears, and twenty-two by western mortgagees who foreclosed the mortgages. Many property owners could not pay their taxes during the Depression, and no one purchased properties at Tax Sales.[12] Consequently, the City was also in debt, as it had acquired too many properties, which had become virtually valueless.

Repossession of Properties, 1940s – 1960s

After the outbreak of the second Sino-Japanese War in 1937, remittances to China became impossible. As a result, there was a gradual accumulation of capital in the Chinese community. A few operators of gambling clubs in Chinatown made a fortune during the war. Taking advantage of the property market stagnation in the 1940s, they started buying properties in Chinatown again. Meanwhile, some hard-working merchants who were born and educated in Victoria either rebuilt their families' declining businesses or ventured into new enterprises. They had enough savings, or pooled their savings, to buy back properties from the City. Chinatown properties that were worth tens of thousands of dollars before the 1930s depression could be bought in the 1940s for a few thousand dollars. In 1920, for example, Gim Ging and Lee Ward had purchased a brick building on Cormorant Street for $22,500, losing it to the City for tax arrears in 1938. In January 1941, James Lim bought the building from the City for only $1,770.[13] These low market values for real estate encouraged the Chinese to buy Chinatown properties again. During the 1940s, the Chinese purchased twenty-one lots in Blocks E, L, and M, either from the City or from Caucasian owners. In the following decade, the Lou-Poy brothers of the Pioneer Fruit and Vegetable Company were the most significant investors in Chinatown, purchasing eight contiguous lots in the western half of Block F and two lots in Block B. Property purchases by several Chinese families and groups of Chinese partners from the 1940s through the 1960s established the basic Chinese land ownership pattern found in Chinatown today (Fig. 12).

Summary

The records of property owners were very difficult to locate, assemble, and interpret. Incomplete or missing documents made interpretation difficult, if not impossible. Different types of records compounded the problem, as did the English recording of Chinese personal names. In spite of these difficulties, the ownership of each lot of land in Chinatown was traced by delving into hundreds of conveyances, tax sale records, assessment rolls, and other documents in the Land Registry Office and the Provincial Archives in Victoria. An analysis of Chinese ownership patterns in the past 134 years revealed that the earliest land investors were a few wealthy merchants who had come to Victoria from San Francisco. At the turn of the twentieth century, various associations and numerous local merchants became the principal property owners in Chinatown. This radical shift in the ownership pattern reflected the demise of large-scale businessmen after the gold rushes.

Documental records showed that most of the Chinese owners did not have much capital to acquire properties. They had relied on

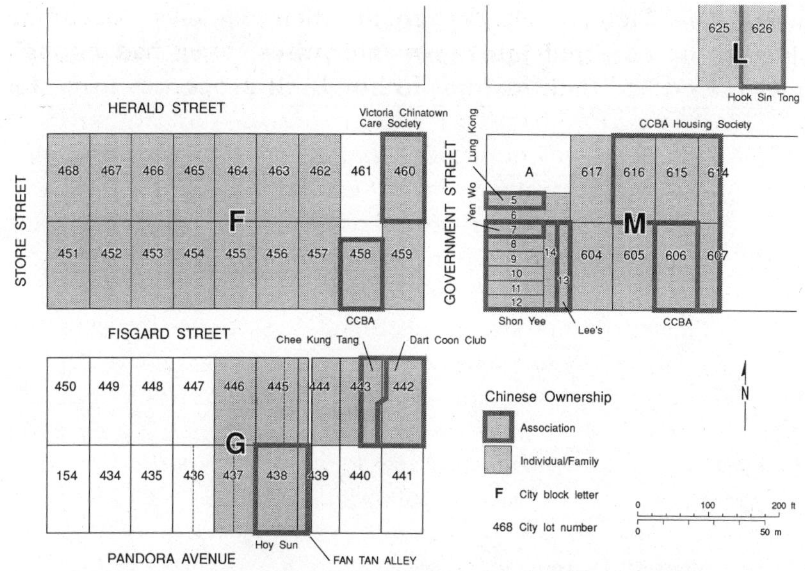

Fig. 12. Chinese-owned properties in Chinatown, March 1991.

large loans or mortgages; many of them, therefore, lost their properties through defaulting on loan or tax payments during the economic depression of the 1930s. After the Second World War, a new group of Chinese property owners emerged, including a few gambling operators and several second-generation merchants who either inherited properties from their families or purchased land directly from the City or from Caucasian owners. Today, these family groups and voluntary associations are the major Chinese landlords of Chinatown, reflecting the adaptation of traditional norms to a Western system of property ownership and transmission.

To a certain degree, Chinese property ownership has been a response to the physical extent of the Chinese community, playing an important role in sustaining the Oriental characteristics of Chinatown buildings. Chinese associations, restaurants, and other business concerns are set within a colourful townscape full of decorative and structural Oriental forms. The survival of Chinatown streetscapes depends much on these Chinese institutions and businesses, which in turn are more viable if they are the property owners as well.

Table 3
Sale of Lots on Esquimalt Harbour, 12 July 1858

Successful Bidders	*Lot Number*	*Bidding Price*
7 Chinese Bidders		
Ah Gi	54	$1,450
Ah So	55	975
Ah Tun	52	775
Li Hing	53	675
Ah Tin	48	675
Ah Foo	49	650
Ah Pow	50	600
10 Non-Chinese Bidders		
P.C. Dart	57	$1,225
P.C. Dart	56	1,050
Montead	28	675
Livinsky	47	600
N. Carroll & Co.	51	550
N. Carroll & Co.	11	550
N. Carroll & Co.	12	550
C. Bartlett	43	450
C. Bartlett	44	450
Dr. Turnbull	24	450
Dr. Turnbull	25	450
Livinsky	23	425
Dr. Turnbull	20	400
Higgins	27	400
C. Eastman	22	400
Livinsky	26	375
Waddington	45	375
A. Sherro	21	350

Source: The Victoria Gazette, *14 July 1858.*

«3» East Meets West

The miners are still going and coming all the time. Chinamen are crowding in very rapidly... Anon you meet throngs of Chinamen packing up the river. They pass and greet you in broken English with, "how you do John". We are all Johns to them, and they to us. Their bamboo canes and heavy loads are strangely singular to us.[1]

* * *

A procession of moon-eyed Orientals... on their way to the wharf of the steamer for Langley. The display consisted of sixteen individuals, whose manoeuvres, although accomplished in Indian file, caused quite a scattering of bystanders on the line of march, as each of the immigrating army was his own pack animal and was loaded in true Chinese style, with a pole on the shoulder, dangling from each end of which were packages of provisions.[2]

* * *

The American bark... sailed yesterday for Hong Kong... with 12 Chinamen.... One of the above-mentioned happy-go-lucky Johns informed us that with $500 in cash, he could live in China five or six years, during which he would drink good tea, smoke opium, and visit all his

> *Celestial cousins, and then have sufficient left... to come back. Two of the Johns intend "returning in the spring", bringing their families of female Johns and demi-Johns with them.*[3]

The foregoing excerpts from a local newspaper reveal how the Chinese were viewed by westerners during the gold rush in undeveloped British Columbia. In any language contact situation, there is bound to be confusion, misunderstanding, and frustration. Western people found it difficult or did not bother to struggle to pronounce or spell Chinese names. They called the Chinese "Johns," "John Chinamen," "Orientals," "Celestials," "Mongolians," "Chinks," and other derisive names. Similarly, Chinese people found it difficult, if not impossible, to pronounce or spell Western names, let alone establish a man's identity. Lee Sing, for example, a Chinese restaurant owner, declared bankruptcy and submitted to the court a list of thirty-one persons who owed him a total of $540 for meals. The debtors were all non-Chinese, and were listed as "Lean Man White Man, $20; French Old Man, $8.00; Get Tight Man, $7.5; Indian Joe, $10.00; Fat Frenchman, $30.62; Lame Leg Man, $40; Red Whiskers, $18.50; Captain of Schooner, $50; Shoemaker, gone to California, $15; Red Shirt Man, $27 . . . ."[4] Undoubtedly, this list posed a perplexing problem for the judge in identifying the debtors. The linguistic barrier between the two cultures also resulted in peculiar Chinese names in the Chinese society.

Origins of John Chinaman

Why were Chinese commonly called Johns in those days? There are no certain answers. Since the early Chinese immigrants had difficulty pronouncing English names, and since "John" was easy to pronounce and was commonly used by English-speaking people, the Chinese may have greeted every person of European extraction with, "How do you do, John?" On the other hand, the Caucasians were also puzzled by Chinese names and had trouble identifying one Chinese from another. Instead of making an effort to pronounce a Chinese name, the white people may have called every Chinese "John." Thus, the Chinese were all Johns to Western people, and Western people were all Johns to the Chinese!

There may be another explanation, however. In the old days, an Indian was referred to as a "siwash"; it is said to be a variant of the French "sauvage."[5] It is thus possible that the English "John" might be a corruption of the French "jaune" (meaning yellow). The Frenchmen may have called the Chinese people "jaune Chinoise" (yellow Chinese), which gradually became John Chinamen.[6]

Ah Chin

Chinese residents in Victoria were listed in the 1869 Mallandaine's Victoria Directory as Ah Caha, Ah Chin, Ah Ching, Ah Coo, and so on. For euphony, Chinese people in South China commonly prefix the syllable "Ah" to the name of a close friend or junior. If a Chinese man is named Wu Ming, for example, his close friends may address him as Ah Wu (the family name) or Ah Ming (the first name). In North China, the single syllable "Xiao" (Little) or "Lao" (Old) is substituted. Hence, Xiao Ming or Lao Wu may be used. The aspirating syllable "Ah" is used only colloquially and is never written as part of a name. Unfamiliar with the Chinese custom, Western people tended to treat "Ah" as part of a Chinese name.

Official records suggest that the spelling of Chinese names must have been a great puzzle for Western people in those days. In the Land Registry Office in Victoria, there are a few old deeds on which the names of property owners were changed several times, possibly because of misspellings. The owners of one property, for example, were first written as Chang Foon Hung, Chin Fong Hong, and Sou Hong Ho. These names were crossed out and replaced by Chin Foon Hung, Chin Foon Hong, and Sou Kong Ho. These spellings were crossed out yet again. Eventually, all of the corrections were struck out and replaced with the simple phrase, "Owned by 3 Chinamen."

Similarly, instead of striving to spell out Chinese names, the registrar of the Ross Bay Cemetery started on 18 March 1873 to record the Chinese who were interred there by simply writing "Chinaman No. 1," "Chinaman No. 2," and so on.[7] It was not until 4 October 1880 that Chinese names were used in the Burial Records.

Systems of Transliteration

The spelling of Chinese names confuses not only Westerners, but also the Chinese themselves, because of the different dialects, surname origins, and systems of transliteration. Prior to 1958, the two widely recognized systems of transliteration were the Postal system, used by the Chinese Postal Authorities, and the Wade-Giles system, which was developed by Thomas F. Wade and Herbert A. Giles, former British diplomats in China.[8] The spellings by these two systems are very different. Peking, Tsingtao, and Soochow, for example, which are the Postal system spellings, will be romanized as Pei-ching, Ch'ing-tao, and Su-chou respectively according to the Wade-Giles system.

In 1956 the Chinese government began to devise a new phonetic alphabet for the transliteration of Chinese characters. On 11 February 1958, the government announced the Pinyin system (meaning the "Spelling the Sounds" system) and adopted it as the official transliteration system. In this system, spellings are pronounced as they look – Beijing and Suzhou, for example. There are some exceptions, however. The "c" in the Pinyin system is pronounced like "ts," and "q" is pronounced like "ch." Hence the surname Ts'ai is transliterated as Cai, and the dynasty Ch'ing is transliterated as Qing. In some cases, when the vowel or consonant break is unclear, an apostrophe is used to aid in pronunciation, as in the cities Xi'an (not Xian) and Yan'an (not Yanan). In August 1977, the United Nations Conference on the Standardization of Geographical Names accepted China's request to adopt the Pinyin system as the international standard for transliteration of place names. On 26 September 1978, China announced that the Pinyin system of spelling names and places would supplant various old spelling systems.[9] Since then, the former spellings of such names as China, Mao Tse-tung, and Teng Hsiao-p'ing have been replaced by Zhongguo, Mao Zedong, and Deng Xiaoping respectively. Many overseas Chinese still retain the original spellings of their names. In Canada, it is not uncommon to find different spellings of the same Chinese surname, based on local dialects. The surname Chan, for example, is used by Cantonese, Chen by Taiwanese, Tan by Fujian people, and Tran by Vietnamese Chinese (Fig. 13).

Confusion of Chinese Surnames

The origins of some Chinese surnames in Victoria are fascinating. Four brothers of a Chow family in Victoria, for example, have two different spellings of their surname: John and Bill were surnamed Joe, but their brothers, Ed and Tom, were surnamed Chow. This was caused by the fact that their father had different interpreters fill

Surname	System of Transliteration			
	Postal	Wade Files	Pinyin	Others
陳	*Chan*	*Ch'en*	*Chen*	*Chin, Tan, Tran*
張	*Cheung*	*Chang*	*Zhang*	*Cheong, Truong*
趙	*Chiu*	*Chao*	*Zhao*	*Chew, Trieu*
周	*Chow*	*Chou*	*Zhou*	*Joe, Jow, Joh*
關	*Kwan*	*Kuan*	*Guan*	*Quon, Quan, Touang*
林	*Lam*	*Lin*	*Lin*	*Lem, Lum, Lamb*
劉	*Lau*	*Liu*	*Liu*	*Low, Lowe, Hope*
雷	*Lui*	*Lei*	*Lei*	*Lou, Louie*
馬	*Mah*	*Ma*	*Ma*	*Mar, Marr*
吳	*Ng*	*Wu*	*Wu*	*Eng, Ing, Ngo, Goh*
黃	*Wong*	*Huang*	*Huang*	*Brown, Huynh*

Fig. 13. Different systems of spelling Chinese surnames.

in the application forms for his children's birth certificates; each interpreter had his own method of transliteration.[10]

A Chinese-Canadian may have two surnames, one well known to the public, the other known only to his or her relatives or close Chinese friends. This is due to Western people's ignorance of Chinese customs. In the early days, many Westerners did not know that the Chinese wrote their surnames first and given names last; the given name might consist of one or two characters. For example, if a Chinese was surnamed *Luk* and his given name was Kam Sang, he would write and speak his name as *Luk* Kam Sang, not Kam Sang *Luk* as a Westerner would. When his children attended school, they would tell their English teachers that their father was called *Luk* Kam Sang.[11] Their teachers would think they were surnamed *Sang*, and record it as such. As a result, the children today bear the surname *Sang* instead of *Luk*. The older children, however, may use their real surname, *Luk*, when they speak in Chinese with their Chinese friends.

There is another reason why a Chinese-Canadian may have two different surnames. During the 1950s, discriminatory immigration regulations forced prospective Chinese immigrants to buy the birth certificates of deceased people with living relatives in Canada, and enter Canada with the deceased persons' identification papers. These immigrants were known as "paper sons."[12] If the deceased person was surnamed Hong, and the "paper son" was surnamed Chow, the latter would have two surnames. He would use Hong as his legal surname, but he might continue to use his real surname Chow in Chinese-Canadian circles.

In the case of Mrs. Bessie Tang, a prominent community leader in Victoria, the origin of her surname is different. Her maiden name is Hope, although her real surname is Liu. Her father, a tailor, was called Liu Dun Bao, but Western people always addressed him as Charles Hope. Accordingly, he named his store Charles Hope & Co., and his children's surname became Hope instead of Liu.[13] A search of the Victoria city directories revealed that Chinese tailors in those days were commonly called Charlie by Western people. A Chinese tailor called Charlie probably had to add another name in order to be distinguished from other "Charlies." In the Victoria City Directory of 1912, for example, five tailors are listed: Bo Charley tailor, Charlie Bo tailor, Charlie Hope & Co., Charlie Hoy tailor, and Charlie Wah tailor.[14] In the 1919 City Directory, the three tailoring stores are called Charlie Hope & Co. ladies' and men's tailors, Charlie Wo & Co. tailors, and Bo Charlie tailor.[15] The owners of these three stores were in fact brothers surnamed Liu, but the public knew them by their stores' names. Hence, the three brothers became known as Charlie Hope, Charlie Wo, and Charlie Bo, and had different surnames.

Some Chinese coined their English surnames for the convenience of their Western customers or friends. Wong Pei

Nan's elder brother, for example, decided to use an English name to represent his Chinese name.[16] The Chinese character "Wong" is identical to the Chinese character "yellow" both in script and in Cantonese tone. Wong Pei Nan's elder brother mistakenly thought the English word "brown" meant the colour yellow. Accordingly, he changed his surname from Wong to Brown and chose a Christian name for his younger brother; thus Wong Pei Nan became known as George Brown.

Some Chinese surnames were transliterated like English surnames in an attempt to bypass racial discrimination. In August 1878, the Legislature of British Columbia passed a resolution that "Chinese should not be employed upon the public works of the Province, and that a clause should be inserted in the specifications of all contracts awarded, to the effect that contractors will not be permitted to employ Chinese labour upon the work, and that in the event of their doing so the Government will not be responsible for payment of contract."[17] A Chinese old-timer told me that his grandfather used the surname Lamb instead of Lam because he found it easier to get employment or a contract by using an English surname. His assertion is supported by an incident in August 1922, when Charles Kent, a Chinese tailor, submitted the lowest bid and won the contract from the Liberal government at Ottawa to make uniforms for the quarantine staff and other federal branches in Victoria.[18] When organized labour protested, the Liberals in Victoria said by way of apology that the federal authorities "must have been misled by the name Kent and did not connect it with anyone of Oriental extraction."

Most Chinese surnames have a single character, but two-character surnames are by no means rare; Situ, Ouyang, Sima, Zhuge, Shangguan, and Gongsun are common two-character surnames. A few Chinese bear double-barrelled surnames that in fact represent single-character surnames in Chinese. The surname Ho-Pui, for example, is Ho in Chinese.[19] James Ho was a prominent Chinese merchant in Victoria, but there was another Chinese person bearing the same name. In order to avoid confusion, James Ho decided to adopt his father's full name, Ho Pui, as a surname and changed his name to James Ho-Pui.

Ng is a common Chinese surname in Hong Kong, but this transliterated word is difficult, if not impossible, for Western people to pronounce. Accordingly, many Ng clansmen in Canada prefix the vowel "e" or "i" to their surnames, becoming Eng or

Ing. However, this surname is transliterated as Go or Goh by many Chinese immigrants from Singapore or Malaysia because of their Fujian dialect.

Names of Chinese Stores

Because Westerners found Chinese names difficult to spell, they tended to use the familiar store names for their Chinese owners or operators. Lee Chong, for example, was the manager of Kwong Lee & Co., which was the largest import and export company in Victoria during the gold rush era. He was popularly known as "Kwong Lee" to the Western public instead of "Lee Chong."[20]

As with surnames, a Chinese store may have two names, one well known to Westerners and the other to the Chinese themselves. Marwon Agencies Ltd., an insurance agent in Chinatown, is known to the Chinese as Lee Tung Chong, and the Wing's Market as Fook On Wing. These Chinese store names are not only rarely known to the Western public, but also unknown to many new Chinese immigrants or locally born Chinese residents in Victoria.

In naming their stores, most Chinese merchants in the old days tended to choose certain characters that bore the connotation of prosperity, wealth, affluence, or perpetuity. For example, "Chong," "Lung," and "Hing" mean prosperous, abundant, or flourishing (of the business); "Tai" means extensive, exalted or big-sized (of the shop); "Kwong" means broad, widespread, or wide sale (of the merchandise); "Wing" means perpetual or lasting (of the business); "On" means secure; "Lee" means profit; "Wo" or "Hop" mean harmonious, united, or cooperative (of the partnership); "Yuen" means source (of wealth). Hence, "Kwong Lee" means extensive and prosperous, and "On Hing" means secure and flourishing. In 1884, fifty out of sixty-three Chinese store names included one or more of these eleven Chinese characters (Table 4, pg. 33). "Kee," meaning trademark or sign, was commonly used by small retailers. The last word of the name of a herbalist's store was usually "Tong," meaning hall, as in Po Gee Tong, Jan Yuk Tong, and Man Yuk Tong.

Summary

The great variety of transliterated surnames of Chinese-Canadians is a good example of the way in which Chinese traditional culture was modified as a result of contact with the more powerful Western culture. Early Chinese immigrants had to learn

光緒十年域多利華人商店名錄			
昌 Chong	泰.隆.廣 Tai, Lung, Kwong	興.源.利.永 Hing, Yuen, Lee, Wing	和.安.合.記.堂 Wo, On, Hop, Kee, Tong
1. 泰昌	17. 泰源	33. 廣利	49. 泗和
2. 怡昌泰	18. 泰和	34. 廣祥盛	50. 生和
3. 廣昌	19. 泰巽	35. 廣福	51. 森記
4. 荣昌隆	20. 乾泰	36. 安興	52. 炳記
5. 宏昌隆	21. 泰益	37. 正興	53. 安記
6. 錦昌隆	22. 錦联泰	38. 華興	54. 保記
7. 永昌和	23. 泰来	39. 廣興	55. 福記
8. 永昌	24. 泰興隆	40. 宝源	56. 宝芝堂
9. 源昌	25. 源隆	41. 華源	57. 贊育堂
10. 昌合	26. 義和隆	42. 錦源	58. 合吉
11. 安昌	27. 泗和隆	43. 成源	59. 謙益
12. 联昌	28. 泗隆	44. 同利	60. 綸盛
13. 兆昌	29. 廣安隆	45. 成利	61. 錦華
14. 悦昌	30. 廣安泰	46. 全利	62. 建茂
15. 義昌	31. 廣泰	47. 永祥	63. 美香
16. 協昌	32. 廣荣泰	48. 永安	

Table 4. A list of Chinese stores in Chinatown, 1884.

the language and social customs of the host society, and thus adopted names that Western people could pronounce or remember easily. However, they still retained their ethnic consciousness and continued to use their Chinese names among themselves. Canadian-born Chinese children have sometimes inherited their surnames without knowing how they originated.

« 4 » *Tunnels of the Forbidden Town*

Here, behind dark, dreary stores are darker, drearier rooms where crowds of Chinese can be accommodated at night; and behind these again are shacks and hovels... the theatre is a large, barrack-like place, reached through several alleys.... The police raid these haunts (gambling dens) periodically; and quite recently they were led throughout the length of an entire block in pursuit of a number of flying queues whose owners had not been quite quick enough in making their escapes.

Underneath Chinatown is a perfect maze of secret passages designed for the escape of the white and yellow gamblers... Since the Chinese own all the land on which they build, the authorities can do nothing to prevent this burrowing, with all its dangerous possibilities.[1]

This is an excerpt from a journalist's article about Chinatown in 1911. In those days, the white community portrayed Chinatown as a dangerous and mysterious slum of numerous subterranean passages leading to brothels, opium shacks, and gambling dens. These tunnels were used to smuggle into Chinatown everything from opium to girl slaves to whatever was created by the imaginations of scandal-mongers.

The Myth of Tunnels

Stories about Chinatown's tunnels spread by word of mouth and became the talk of the town. One of these stories was that at night, opium was shipped to the Inner Harbour near the foot of the Johnson Street bridge and then smuggled into Chinatown via a tunnel; the entrance to the tunnel can still be seen at low tide. Another story was that a large tunnel was discovered in the 1950s by members of a city crew during an excavation near Chinatown; the Chinese used this secret passage to smuggle alcohol into Chinatown during the Prohibition from 1917 to 1921. Like other stories, this story has never been substantiated.

A study of the City's storm drain system and interviews with the City's engineer have dispelled the rumour of Chinatown's secret tunnels.[2] During excavation work in the late 1950s, members of a city crew discovered a large water cistern about five feet beneath the road surface of Store Street near Chinatown (Fig. 14). This huge semi-circular structure was about ten feet high, twenty-four feet long, and twenty feet wide at its base. In the early days, it was used by firemen for water storage. Similar cisterns were also found in other parts of the city. When the water cistern was uncovered, some members of the crew thought they had found one of Chinatown's underground tunnels. The news spread, and was modified and dramatized.

About seven feet below the cistern was a large storm drain about four feet in diameter, which ran south along Store Street and then turned west along Johnson Street to the waterfront. Immediately beneath the storm drain was a system of small drains. One drain, about three feet in diameter, followed the direction of the old Johnson Street ravine to the harbour. The entrance of the "tunnel" is in fact an outfall of a storm drain. Indeed, contrary to popular myth, there are no tunnels in Victoria's Chinatown.

Escape Routes

Behind the commercial facades of old buildings was the labyrinthine section of the Forbidden Town, where narrow walkways criss-crossed the area. Weird and horrific tales of

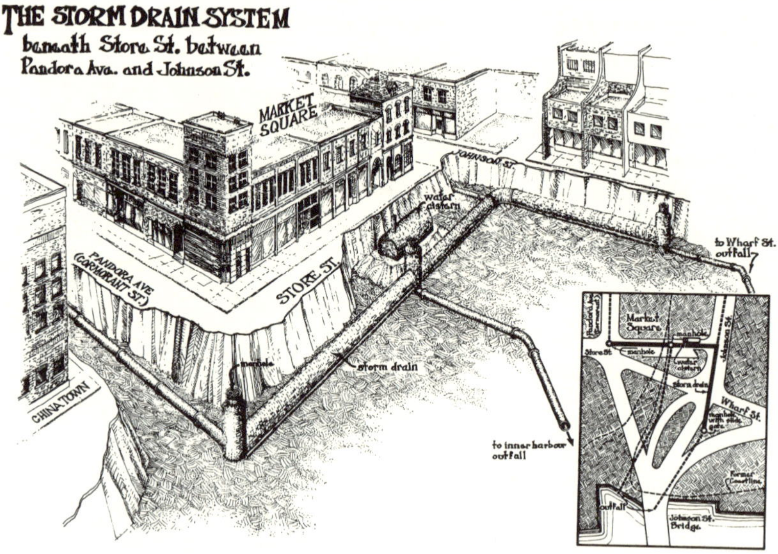

Fig. 14. The storm drain system beneath Store Street.

happenings in this mysterious enclave were often told. A writer recalled one of these tales:

> *We can remember one alley which was barred by a gate having a round hole in it, like the window of a convent door. Underneath this was a very noticeable stain, and a gruesome story accounted for it. A Chinese pursued by an enemy had stuck his head out of the aperture to see if he were safe, only to have it chopped off by said enemy. And nothing could ever remove the stain. Told to us in our impressionable and credulous days, the memory of our horror at the sight is still very vivid to us. It was probably quite untrue.*[3]

The Chinese were talented at contriving secret hideouts and hidden routes within the Forbidden Town. For example, many buildings had narrow, covered passageways leading to interior courtyards; a series of wooden doors or iron gates was installed along the lengths of these alleyways. Once a person entered such an alley and closed the entrance door, it was nearly impossible to know where he or she had gone, because the alley had many exits on both sides. Some of these alleys still exist today in

Chinatown buildings. At one time, a building on Fan Tan Alley had a washroom with two doors, one opening to the interior, the other to Fan Tan Alley. Once a person entered a washroom, he or she could "disappear" through the other door. A building on Herald Street that was fitted with an ingenious device for escape still stands today. The rooms on the second floor are all partitioned by two adjoining closets (Fig. 15). The divider of each closet is a concealed door that allows a person to enter one room and "disappear" into another. Another clever escape device is found in the attic of a building on Government Street. The attic is closed by barred windows, but the bars of one window can be removed by pushing a hidden latch to one side; the window will then open to the outside.

In the old days, the police did not want to stop gambling, but they tried to control it, periodically raiding Chinatown. The newspaper usually reported these raids and arrests with relish. To make it difficult for the police to get in, operators installed one door after another along an alley leading to the gambling clubs. When a lookout spotted the police through a peephole, he would immediately pull a rope or release a spring that dropped a heavy door into place. Thus the operators had time to destroy the evidence and let gamblers leave via the escape routes. In order to secure evidence and arrest gamblers, police raiding Chinatown usually armed themselves with mallets, axes, or hatchets for breaking down the doors and partitions of Chinese residences. The police did not treat the white gambling clubs in the Broad Street neighbourhood in the crude manner applied to the Chinese. Andrew McGavin was probably one of the very few police commissioners who opposed the treatment dispensed to the Chinese. He once remarked that the method police used to raid the Chinese gambling dens "is a disgrace to any civilized community."[4]

There was another reason why the Chinese often had to escape police raids in those days. The City Council had passed a so-called "cubic air" bylaw specifically designed to prohibit too many Chinese people from sharing a room. According to this bylaw, each room should contain at all times at least 384 cubic feet of space for each occupant, and should have a window, made to open, at least two feet square.[5] A room measuring eight feet square and six feet high, for example, should not have more than one occupant. Since the poor Chinese could not afford to rent a room for just one person, they continued to live together

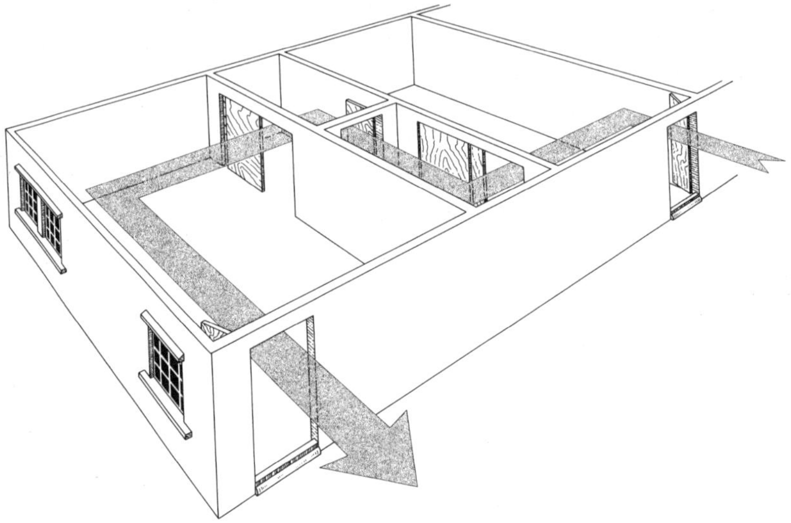

Fig. 15. Two rooms separated by two adjoining closets.

and share the expenses of renting, in defiance of the bylaw. Thus the police frequently came to their living quarters, arrested them, and fined them for overcrowding. The fines became an attractive source of income for the City, encouraging the police to make more arrests.

This restrictive bylaw not only caused much financial hardship on the poor Chinese residents, it frequently disturbed their home lives and privacy. Eventually, on 2 November 1893, the Chinese Consolidated Benevolent Association (CCBA), a representative organization of the Chinese in Victoria, was forced to pass a resolution stating that any Chinese resident arrested during a police raid and sentenced to a fine for overcrowding should go to jail instead of paying a fine.[6] After he was released, he would be rewarded with $10 by the Association. If he paid a fine to the police, he would be fined $10 by the Association for disobedience. This was one of the passive Chinese means of ending the raids. A Chinese old-timer stated that soon after the CCBA enforced its resolution, the police came to living quarters in Chinatown and again made arrests for overcrowding. The Chinese lawbreakers all pleaded guilty and accepted jail sentences, which took the police completely by surprise. If all of the Chinese offenders were thrown into jail, they could not be accommodated by the small police cells. Furthermore, the police themselves would violate the bylaw, because the city jail was not big enough to accommodate the Chinese at 384 cubic feet per person. Eventually, all of the offenders were released. From that time on, the police stopped raiding Chinatown for overcrowding and let the offensive "cubic air" bylaw lapse.

Summary

Myths are beliefs, perceptions, and attitudes resulting from unsubstantiated stories that are usually created and passed from one generation to another by an unconscious, non-rational process. Eventually, people begin to believe them. Many Chinatown myths involve made-up things that have nothing to do with reason and understanding. A recent newspaper article, written by Maureen O'Dea, is a good example of a made-up story that might become another myth of Chinatown (Appendix I).

This chapter contrasts the tunnel myth with the escape reality; the former is mistaken, unreal and false; the latter is understandable, real and true. In the past, the police constantly raided Chinatown for overcrowding, gambling, and prostitution, very often manhandling the offenders. The Chinese had to devise secret hideouts and escape routes as a passive means of protecting themselves against the police harassment. Once a Chinese entered the Forbidden Town and lurked in an internal courtyard via an escape route, it would be impossible for his pursuers to find him. Thus many people began to believe that there must be one or more tunnels inside Chinatown. As the story was passed on from one person to another, it eventually became a myth. This fantasy about a Chinatown tunnel is still repeated today, and sometimes exaggerated, by tourist guides and other narrators who wish to intrigue their listeners.

«5» *Fan Tan and Fan Tan Alley*

> *Gambling is, par excellence, the Chinese amusement. That Coolie is poor indeed who cannot scrape together a few cents to lose or double at chuck-luck or fantan.*[1]

In the early days, Chinese labourers had to work very long hours to eke out a living in Canada. Nevertheless, they were not behind people of other ethnic groups in their love of amusements. For relaxation, the tired and lonely labourers took part in outdoor activities in Chinatown, such as theatre-going, lion-dancing parades, temple visits, celebrations of the Chinese New Year, and other festivals. Indoor entertainments included playing Chinese musical instruments, practising martial arts, holding chess contests, reading Chinese newspapers and magazines, and playing games of cards and dominoes. Fan Tan was by far the most popular indoor entertainment in Chinatown.

Fan Tan

Fan Tan, a gambling game which originated in China, was once very popular in Chinatown's gambling dens, commonly referred to as "Fan Tan Guan" (Fan Tan clubs). "Fan" means to turn over

Fig. 16. Fan Tan game.

(a cup), and "Tan" means to spread out (a pile of buttons); hence the name of the game. It is played on a square cardboard at the end or in the centre of a table. The sides of the cardboard are assigned four numbers: the side nearest the croupier is one, his right-hand side is two, the opposite side three, and his left-hand four (Fig. 16). The players bet on the numbers: if a player places all his stakes on the side, he bets on that number to win, and if he places his bets exactly at a corner between two sides, he bets on either number to win. The gambling club acts as the "bank," and its croupier pays three to one on bets placed on the side and even money on bets at the corner if either number wins. He takes a percentage of all the stakes. In Victoria's Chinatown, the rake-off was usually between seven and ten percent.

At the start of the game, the dealer takes a random handful of white buttons or beads and covers them with a little bowl-shaped brass cup. After players have placed their bets, the dealer lifts the cup and spreads out the pile of buttons with a tapered bamboo stick with a bow at the end. Then the dealer deftly counts off the buttons from the pile, four at a time, with the curved stick. All groups of fours are disregarded; the number of buttons left in the last batch determines the winner. If Player A has placed $10 on two, for example, and Player B $10 on the corner between two and three, both players will lose if the last group contains one or four buttons. If the last batch contains three buttons, Player A will lose, but Player B will receive $9 if the rake-off is ten percent. If the last batch contains two buttons, then Player A will get $27 and Player B $9 after the rake-off.

Fan Tan Alley

This alley is a narrow lane linking Cormorant Street (now known as Pandora Avenue) and Fisgard Street (Fig. 17). It runs through lots 439 and 444 in City Block G, dividing the two adjoining lots into about one-third on their western portions and two-thirds on their eastern portions. In June 1881, William J. Macdonald purchased the eastern two-thirds of Lot 439 from Bejamin Healy for $5,500. In the following year he built a brick building on the site; this building is referred to hereafter as the Macdonald Building (see Fig. 54). It was leased to the Chinese until it was sold in January 1908 to Lim Bang, Wong Yock, and Wong Tong for $10,500.[2] In 1884, Loo Chew Fan, one of the owners of Kwong Lee & Co., purchased Lot 438 and the western one-third of Lot 439, on which he built a large brick building referred to hereafter as the Loo Chew Fan Building[3] (see Fig. 53). The Macdonald and Loo Chew Fan buildings were separated by a narrow lane of about four feet, which provided an access from Cormorant Street to Fisgard Street. Behind these two brick buildings were several wood-frame structures housing Kwong Lee and Tai Soong opium factories.

In June 1887, Sheam Tip and Low Yan San purchased Lot 445 and the western one-third of Lot 444. In the following year they built a brick building about twenty feet wide on the western one-third of Lot 444. In 1901 Lee Mong Kow, a government interpreter and a prominent community leader, added a brick

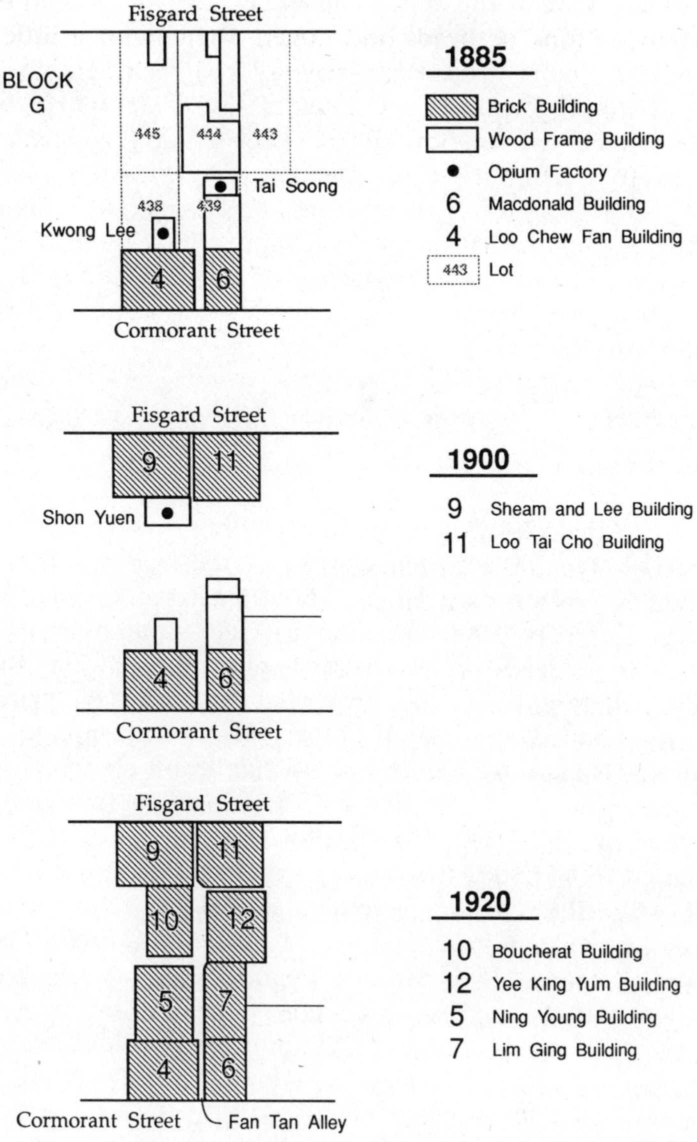

Fig. 17. The formation of Fan Tan Alley, 1885 – 1925.

building to Sheam's building and the two were combined as one, referred to hereafter as the Sheam and Lee Building (see Fig. 56). In March 1892, Loo Tai Cho purchased the western two-thirds of Lot 444 and the western half of Lot 443, and built a brick

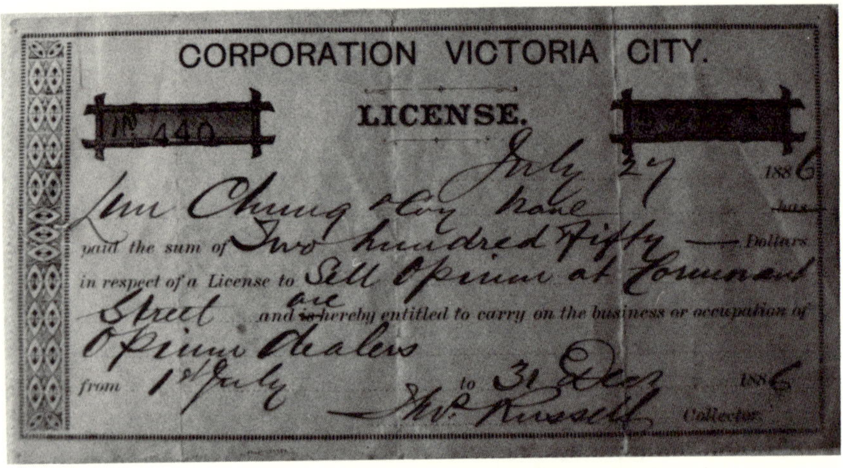
CORPORATION VICTORIA CITY.

No. 440

LICENSE.

July 27 1886

Lum Chung & Coy have

paid the sum of Two hundred Fifty — Dollars

in respect of a License to Sell Opium at Cormorant

Street and are hereby entitled to carry on the business or occupation of

Opium dealers

from 1st July to 31 Decr 1886

Thos. Russell Collector.

Fig. 18. An opium licence issued by the City of Victoria, 1886.

building in the following year. This building, referred to hereafter as the Loo Tai Cho Building, was separated from the Sheam and Lee Building by a narrow lane of about three feet (see Fig. 58).

In the early 1900s, the Shon Yuen Opium Factory was housed in a wooden structure behind the Sheam and Lee Building. Before 1908, the provincial and federal governments had not banned the manufacture and sale of opium, mainly because this lucrative industry was a significant source of income for them. The annual licence fee on an opium firm in Victoria was $250 in 1886 (Fig. 18). In 1906, the import duty on opium amounted to $47,500.[4] The opium business was legal until 20 July 1908, when the federal government passed an act to prohibit the importation, manufacture, and sale of opium in Canada.[5] Thus, the remaining four opium factories in Victoria – Shon Yuen, Tai Yune, Quong Man Fung, and Kwong On Lung – were closed.

Between the 1910s and 1920s, four brick buildings were built as infilling structures between the existing brick buildings facing Cormorant and Fisgard streets. In 1912, M. Boucherat built the Boucherat Building, a brick structure that adjoined the Sheam and Lee Building. In the following year, Yee King Yum and Nip Lung Jim built the Yee King Yum Building behind the Loo Tai Cho Building; they were separated by a narrow alley (Fig. 19). In 1920 Ning Young Yee Hing Tong built the Ning Young Building (Fig. 20), an adjoining brick structure to the Loo Chew Fan Building. In the same year, Lim Ging and Lee Ward built the Lim

Fig. 19.
A view of Fan Tan Alley, Boucherat Building on the left, and Yee King Yum Building on the right.

Ging Building behind the Macdonald Building (Fig. 21). Thus by 1920, the eight contiguous brick buildings had formed a 240-feet alley, with a width varying between three and six feet, between Fisgard and Cormorant streets. This long and narrow brick chasm became known to the Chinese as Fan Tan Xiang (Fan Tan Alley) after several Fan Tan Guan (Fan Tan gambling clubs) were operated there during the 1910s. Both ends of the alley were closed by a series of wooden doors. Visitors to the alley were scrutinized by a watchman through a square peephole before the first door was opened to them. The name of the alley was unknown to the white community until a police raid on a gambling den was reported in a local newspaper on 24 January 1916:

Fig. 20.
The Ning Young Building.

> *There were nearly one hundred Chinese taken in the raid which was made on Thursday night on the Oriental club in Fan Tan alley... Sergt. Fry told of the search made of the premises upstairs above 1 and 2 Fan Tan alley, west side.... The first door through which the police had to pass, was unlocked, a second had to be forced open and a third which was barred and bolted, was broken down.*[6]

Fan Tan Alley was listed in the city directory for the first time in 1923. At that time, it consisted of three clubs (Fay Yen Mutual Society, Asiatic Club, and Tai Lee Club), two cafes (New Republic Cafe and Sin Fun Loy Cafe), and a small store called York Kee.[7] Two years later, Tai Lee Club, a Fan Tan club, was sold and renamed Sai Lee Club.

Fig. 21.
The Lim Ging Building.

After Hong Kong was occupied by the Japanese in 1941 and the war continued, the Chinese in Canada could not return to China. Nor could they send remittances to their home villages. As they had some savings and nowhere to spend the money, many Chinese began to indulge in gambling. Throughout the 1940s, Fan Tan Alley was busy and crowded with these lonely single men. In its heyday, Fan Tan Alley had nearly ten Fan Tan clubs.[8] The popular ones included Po Yuen, Fook Luk Shou, Sun Sai Kai, Ta Sai Kai, Ta Guan, Tai Loy, Fook Lee, and Sing Lee. Some of their signs can still be seen on brick columns or on the tops of doors in the alley today (Fig. 22). In addition, there were a few Chinese cafes and small restaurants, such as Kwong Chew Restaurant, Fan's Cafe, and Kam Ma Cafe.

Fig. 22. Signs of Fan Tan clubs.

When the Second World War ended and the Exclusion Act was repealed, Chinese were permitted to sponsor their wives and children to come to Canada. Thus many former bachelors began enjoying family lives instead of spending their leisure time in gambling houses. The gambling clubs in Fan Tan Alley were closed one after another as the police continued to crack down on them and the number of customers declined. By the mid-1960s, only three businesses remained in the alley: Wing Fat Pancakes, Hop Shi Choy Suey, and the Sing Lee Club; Sing Lee was the only remaining Fan Tan club. When the alley premises were condemned in the 1970s, and residents were told to move out, the landlords left the premises vacant, finding it too expensive to renovate them to meet the standards of the new national fire and building codes. As the alley did not perform any commercial function, it was no longer listed in the city directory after the mid-1970s. The exterior facades of buildings on both sides of the alley were much damaged by vandalism, so the landlords boarded up all the doors and windows. Fan Tan Alley was deserted, and became a convenient drinking spot for street alcoholics. The gambling game of Fan Tan also ceased to be played in Chinatown after the 1970s.

When the rehabilitation of Chinatown was launched in 1979, I conceived the concept of an "Atelier Model" for the rehabilitation of buildings in Fan Tan Alley. The objective was to develop the alley into the "Montmartre" of Victoria. I suggested to its property owners that although their condemned buildings were unfit for residence, they could be used by young artists and artisans as studios or workshops. In return for their labour and materials to renovate the premises, the artist tenants could be charged lower rents. Thus, a few artists began to move into Fan Tan Alley.[9] By the summer of 1983, several vacant premises on both sides of the alley had been renovated and rented out to fourteen artisans and artists.[10] They were the pioneers of the "alley art" of Chinatown, which included acrylic paintings, oil paintings, watercolours, charcoal and graphite drawings, clay and bronze sculptures, antique reproductions, and the manufacture and repair of stained glass windows and furniture. Fan Tan Alley was listed again in the city directory in 1987, and included one restaurant, five offices, and eleven stores.[11] Today, Fan Tan Alley is a popular spot frequented by curious tourists. By 1991, more than ten business concerns had been established in the alley.

« 6 » *Tongs and Tong Wars*

> *Fan Tan Alley – a narrow lane that still seems to echo with strange crises in a far-off night tong war – remains dormant.*[1]
>
> * * *
>
> *When the play was over, the horror began. Victoria tongs took awful vengeance. Theatre Alley, like Fan Tan Alley, once ran straight through from Cormorant to Fisgard. It was not always a peaceful spot in the years of the tongs and hatchetmen.*[2]

Such excerpts from newspaper articles can be counted on to stimulate readers. In the old days, rumours and news about tong wars in Chinatown were usually "played up" by Western newspapers. This was due to misunderstandings about the functions of "tongs" and the causes of the rivalry between them.

The Meaning of Tong

The Chinese character "tong" means a hall or a place to meet and talk. A great variety of Chinese organizations, such as clan associations, county associations, business organizations, charitable organizations, and secret societies, are commonly designated as "tongs" and subsumed under this term. Some of these tongs are very important to Chinese immigrants, because they recreate the institutions with which they were familiar in China. In the old days, many of the tongs were important social mechanisms that served the needs of overseas Chinese, helping them adjust to their new lives in white society and giving them a sense of social security in the face of cultural deprivation and socioeconomic exclusion in the host society. Many of the tongs were also integrating mechanisms by which the solidarity of their members was maintained. Each tong helped its own members, irrespective of their wealth and status, and stood behind them whenever they had trouble with the white community or got into disputes with members of other tongs.

Nevertheless, the solidarity of tong members sometimes had a detrimental effect on the Chinese community itself. It often became a dividing force in Chinatown when disputes or conflicts of interest occurred. If, for example, a man quarrelled with another man over a woman or money, and both men called for help from their own tongs, the argument between two individuals might develop into an open fight between two tongs. Occasionally, disputes over the control of gambling dens and prostitutes in Chinatown resulted in murders or violent fights. Traditional hatreds or feuds between one village and another, or between one clan and another in China, were sometimes passed on to the overseas Chinese. For example, open warfare between the Taishan and the Hakka natives in China had been waged for more than half a century. Thus it was not uncommon for a slight conflict between a Taishan native and a Hakka native in Chinatown to quickly stir up enmity between their tongs and end in a so-called "tong war." Hence there were many reasons for inter-tong rivalry, which the white public was usually unaware of.

Classification of Tongs

There are eight major types of tongs: (i) county associations, (ii) clan associations, (iii) dialect associations, (iv) the Hongmen society, (v) political parties, (vi) recreation clubs, (vii) religious groups, and (viii) other organizations such as merchants' associations, alumni organizations, veterans' associations, and charity societies. Heading these groups of associations, societies, and clubs was an umbrella organization known as the Chinese Benevolent Association (CBA).

Many tongs have their own tong buildings in Chinatown. The top floors are usually used as assembly halls and offices, and the lower floors are rented out to generate income. Many of these association buildings, built in the late nineteenth and early twentieth centuries, have rich heritage values, and are integral components of Chinatown's streetscape.

County Associations

A county association is based on the geographical origin of one's ancestral roots, and its members usually speak the same or similar dialects. For example, Yu Hing Tong (now known as the Hoy Sun Ning Yang Benevolent Association) on Pandora Avenue was founded by people of Hoy Sun (or Taishan) county in Guangdong Province, China (Fig. 23). Similarly, Hook Sin Tong on Herald Street was formed by people from Zhong Shan county, and Chong Hou Tong (now known as Yue Shan Society) on Fisgard Street by people from Panyu County. These tongs were called "big county" associations in Victoria because of the size of their memberships. Sometimes, so-called "small county" people banded together in order to form a united association with a larger membership. San Yup Tung Heung Hui (the Three Counties Association), for example, was founded by people from the counties of Nanhai, Shunde, and Hua.

If a Chinese immigrant originated from Zhong Shan county, his Canadian-born children and all of their descendants would still be considered natives of Zhong Shan county. They would be qualified to join either the Hook Sin Tong or the Shon Yee Association, because both clan associations were formed by Zhong Shan people. One exception to this generalization, however, is found in the Shon Yee Association in British Columbia, whose membership is open to any Zhong Shan native provided he or she is not surnamed Lau. In 1925, members of the Shon Yee Association wrangled with those of Qinshan Club of Hook Sin Tong about a campaign fund for the construction of a hospital in Zhong Shan County.[3] The altercation ended in street fights in which three members of the Shon Yee Association were killed by members of the Qinshan Club, most of whom were surnamed Lau. Hence the association passed a resolution that

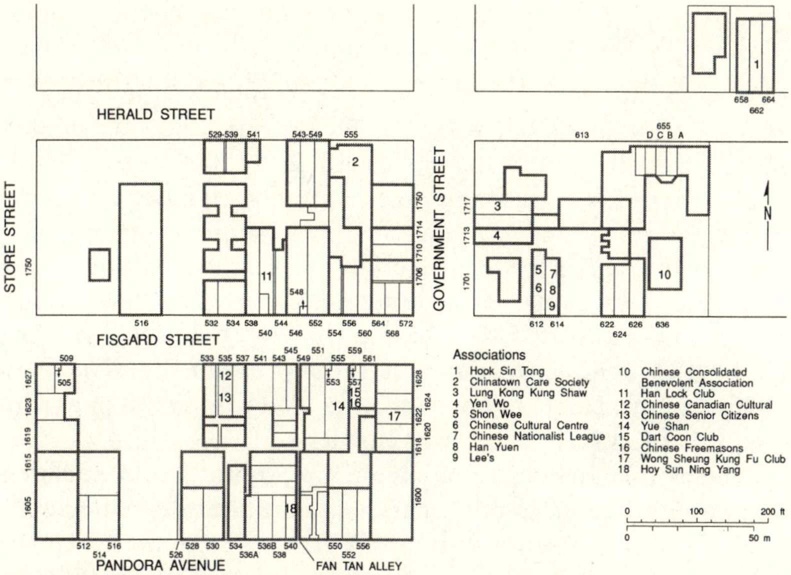

Fig. 23. Locations of Chinese voluntary associations, 1991.

membership should be denied to any Zhongshan native bearing the surnam of Lau. This resolution still stands today.

Dialect Associations

Unlike a county association, a dialect association unites people who speak a similar dialect, even though they may have come to Victoria from different counties. During the Eastern Dynasty, for example, many people migrated from North China to South China, settling down in Wuhua, Huizhou, Chixi, and a few other counties in Guangdong Province. These northern immigrants were called Hakka people (meaning visitors) by the established inhabitants of the province, who called themselves the Bendi people (meaning local natives). The Hakka people all speak the same dialect and practise similar customs, which are completely different from those of the Bendi. In Victoria, the Hakka people formed their own association: Yen Wo Tong (now known as the Yen Wo Society). Tam Kung, their patron saint, is now housed in a shrine on the top floor of their tong building on Government Street.

Clan Associations

A clan association is based on the patrimony from which a person inherits his or her surname. Its members bear a common surname, which is the basis for their "blood relationship." Although they may have come from different counties and speak different dialects, they are united. Their sense of relationship developed through a supposed common remote ancestry. Lung Sai Tong, for example, now known as the Lee's Association, opens membership to all Chinese having the surname Lee. Similarly, Yee Fung Toy Tong was formed by the Yees, Lum Sai Ho Tong by the Lums, Wong Kong Ha Tong by the Wongs, and Chow Oi Lin Kung Shaw by the Chows.

In many clan associations, members are not an independent lineage or lineage segment in the making, because they have not chosen a genealogical point of reference to define themselves as a unit within a larger unit.[4] For example, Ming Yee Tong on Government Street (now known as Lung Kong Kung Shaw or Lung Kong Tin Yee Association) was formed by a group of people who were surnamed Lau, Kwan, Cheung, and Chiu. Their clan relationship is based on the legendary sworn-brotherhood of four heroes of the Three Kingdoms Period (A.D. 220–280): Lau Bei, Kwan Yu, Cheung Fei, and Chiu Tze Lung. Similarly, on the basis of an obscure clan relationship, Gee Tuck Tong was formed by a group of people bearing the surnames Chow, Choy, Ng, Yung, and Cho, and Soo Yuen Tong by the Louies, Kongs, and Fongs.

Clan associations are more numerous than county or dialect associations because there are more than one hundred clans among the Chinese immigrants in Canada. Each clan may have its own association, and different clans may have merged into larger trans-familial and multi-surnamed clan associations.

Hongmen Society

Like the county, dialect, and clan associations, the Hongmen Society (or Triad Society) originated in China. A secret political organization in China, it was established in the 1760s, primarily to overthrow the Manchu regime and restore the Ming Dynasty.[5] The five founders later divided the Society into five lodges, or tongs. One of them was called Hung Shun Tong; many Chinese immigrants to North America were members of this tong. In the United States and Canada, branches of Hung Shun Tong were formed under different names, such as Hip Sing Tong, Bing Kung Tong, Suey Sing Tong, and Chee Kung Tong. Chee Kung Tong in Victoria was founded in 1876. In the old days, these secret societies depended on gambling dens, brothels, and opium joints for their income.

The Hongmen Society played a very important role in Dr. Sun Yat-Sen's success in overthrowing the Manchu regime. Soon after he was sworn in as a member of the Hongmen Society in 1903, he imbued it with his revolutionary ideas and transformed it from a secret society into an open revolutionary party.

Political Parties

As the overseas Chinese in Canada became more conscious of political conditions in China after the turn of the nineteenth century, political organizations began to emerge. The Chinese Empire Reform Association (CERA) was the first Chinese political party established in Chinatown. It was formed by Kang Yu Wei, a brilliant Chinese statesman and scholar. Attempting to save the declining Manchu Empire, he sought to establish a constitutional monarchy like that in Britain and adopt Western science and technology and methods of education.[6] Based on his advice, Emperor Guangxu issued a series of reform edicts in the summer of 1898. Feeling the threat of the reform, Empress Dowager, the Emperor's mother, immediately imprisoned her son, revoked the reform edicts, and started arresting and executing the pro-British reformers. Kang managed to escape to Canada, where in 1899 he mobilized the overseas Chinese to form the CERA as a strong political party to save the Empire and the Emperor. Throughout the 1900s, CERA branches were established in several major Chinatowns across Canada. After the downfall of the Manchu government in 1911, the CERA became known as the Constitutional Party. By the end of the 1910s, the party was defunct.

The Kuomintang (KMT) or Nationalist League, led by Dr. Sun Yat-Sen, developed into a paramount, powerful, political party after the establishment of the Republic of China in 1912. Branches of KMT were set up in Chinatowns throughout North America. Because of its vigorous recruitment of members, the KMT directly challenged the leadership of the Chee Kung Tong

(CKT) in Chinatowns. The CKT members felt that they had been betrayed by Dr. Sun, who had forgotten the contributions of the Hongmen people after his success in the revolution.[7] Discord between the KMT and CKT soon developed into enmity. On 8 October 1916, Hoo Hee and other KMT members assaulted Loo Gee Guia, alias Charlie Bo, and his CKT members.[8] This sparked off tong wars between the two parties throughout the late 1910s, in Victoria and in other Canadian cities.

Many CKT members had also been members of the KMT when the two parties worked together to fight the Northern Warlords in China. Because of the disagreement with the KMT, the CKT leaders decided to "purify" their own party by weeding out those who were still closely associated with the KMT. Accordingly, the headquarters of the Dart Coon Club was established in Victoria in 1915. Membership was open only to CKT members who had been confirmed as dedicated Hongmen people. Branches of the Dart Coon Club were later set up in other Canadian Chinatowns.

In October 1923, an international congress of delegates from CKT chapters throughout the world was held in San Francisco. It was decided at the congress that the CKT be reorganized as a political party named the People's Governing Party (Zhongguo Minzhidang).[9] In 1946, the party was renamed the Hongmen People's Governing Party (Zhongguo Hongmen Minzhidang). Today its members are commonly known as the Chinese Freemasons.

Recreation Clubs and Religious Groups

Only three recreation clubs have clubhouses in Chinatown today. Han Yuen is affiliated with the KMT, and its members are virtually KMT members. The club's most important activity is organizing the annual celebration of the Double Ten Festival on 10 October, the National Day of the Republic of China. Another recreation club is called Han Lock; it operates the Chinese lottery. Its membership includes not only Chinese, but also a few Caucasians. Wong Sheung Kung Fu Club is the only Chinese martial arts club in Chinatown; most of its members are Caucasians. Other recreation or sports clubs that do not have clubhouses include the Chinese Golf Club and the Lotus Dancers' Club.

Initially, Christian organizations were alien to Chinatowns, but gradually they began to play an important part in assisting the Chinese people to assimilate into the host society. The activities of the Methodists and Presbyterians were prominent and significant. Not only did they bring the Christian faith to the Chinese community, they also opened the doors of Western society to many Chinese men and their families. They set up missions and schools in Chinatowns, teaching the Chinese people Christianity, the English language, and Western culture. A Chinese Methodist Church and Chinese Presbyterian Church were built in Chinatown. They sponsored many social and cultural activities, and worked with concerned Chinese citizens to try to wipe out vices such as gambling and prostitution. Furthermore, they opposed the discrimination and ill treatment of the Chinese people in Canada. Due to lack of space and depopulation in Chinatown, the Chinese churches are now situated in other parts of the city: the Chinese Presbyterian Church is located at 816 North Park Street, the Chinese Pentecostal Church at 2215 Dowler Place, and the Chinese Alliance Church at 2845 Gosworth Street.

Other Organizations

In addition to the Chinese organizations mentioned, there was a great variety of other Chinese clubs and societies. The Chinese Canadian Friendship Association (CCFA), for example, was formed in May 1971, after Canada recognized the People's Republic of China on 13 October 1970. Throughout the 1970s, the CCFA sponsored touring troupes from China and organized welcoming parties when Chinese diplomats visited Victoria's Chinatown. The public had always confused the CCFA with the Canada-China Friendship Association because of their identical acronyms, so to avoid the confusion, the CCFA changed its name in 1982 to the Chinese Canadian Cultural Association (CCCA).

The Victoria (Chinatown) Lions Club, established in April 1956, is active not only in the Chinese community, but also in society at large. Since its inauguration it has organized an annual Lantern Festival, similar to the Jewish Hadassa Bazaar, and other fund-raising campaigns for Victorian causes. In recent years many new organizations have been formed, including the University of Victoria Chinese Students' Club, the

Victoria Chinese Cultural Centre Society, and the Victoria Chinese Veterans' Association.

Chinese Consolidated Benevolent Association (CCBA)

The CCBA (Zhonghua Huiguan), established in 1884, functioned as a consulate in Canada before the Manchu government established a consulate in Ottawa in 1909.[10] After the 1910s, it was an umbrella organization with a complex, interlocking directorate consisting of representatives from county, dialect, and clan associations, political parties, church groups, and other clubs and societies. In the past, the CCBA was very powerful and influential. Internally, it acted as a mediator to help solve personal disputes and inter-village or interclan strife, in an effort to prevent inter-association disputes from erupting into violence. It administered a Chinese hospital (Appendix II), a Chinese school (Appendix III), and a Chinese cemetery (Appendix IV) in Victoria. It organized fund-raising campaigns to help local Chinese as well as their fellow countrymen in China. Externally, the CCBA represented the Chinese community, functioning as a spokesman for all the Chinese organizations in Victoria. In the past it led the Chinese community to fight against racial discrimination and oppression by the white society. Today, the CCBA, like Chinese benevolent associations in other Chinatowns, has lost its power as an increasing number of Chinese people are assimilated into Canadian society; they no longer need its service and protection. Nevertheless, the CCBA still remains as a nominal representative of the Chinese community in Victoria.

Summary

The terms "tong" and "tong wars" still throw little light on their functions, causes, or consequences. To the uninformed white community, the term "tong" is merely a synonym for a criminal gang or secret society. To some Chinese people, it is a disparaging word to describe their associations. Even today, an authoritative English dictionary defines the word "tong" as "a secret society or fraternal organization esp. of Chinese in the U.S. formerly notorious for gang warfare."[11] This interpretation of the term is due to a misunderstanding of the considerable range of Chinese voluntary associations in Chinatown, and is, at least in part, due to the fact that the organization, functions, and structures of these associations have changed from time to time.

The traditional Chinese voluntary associations are based on shared county origin, clanship, dialect, occupation, and other cultural traits. Through them, the Chinese can interact with one another and organize their lives together. It was and still is within these social and community contexts that the Chinese cultural traditions brought over by immigrants from Hong Kong and China take root in Chinatown. Thus these tongs still form the underlying community structure of overseas Chinese society.

« 7 » *Joss Houses*

> *Temples or Joss houses secreted themselves at the back of buildings. One climbed endless flights of steps to find them, their really beautiful though bizarre images, their painted signs and paper garlands and their heady smell of spicy incense from the burning joss sticks.*[1]

The word "joss" is a Pidgin English word derived from the Portuguese word "Dios," meaning God.[2] Many of the so-called joss houses in Chinatown are in fact shrines of ancestors or patron saints of different types of associations. Ancestral shrines are installed in Lung Kong Kung Shaw, the Lee's Association, and other clan associations. In Victoria, there are two important temples in which different deities are worshipped.

Tam Kung Temple

Tam Kung Temple is not only the oldest temple in Victoria, but also the oldest in Canada. It is housed today on the top floor of the Yen Wo Association at 1713 Government Street. Ngai Mau Sou, alias Harry Ngai, a custodian of the temple, related the story told to him by his predecessors: in the early 1860s, a Hakka native from Guangdong Province, China, came to Victoria, bringing with him a statuette of the God of Tam Kung.[3] When he left for the Fraser goldmining area, he housed the statuette in a wooden niche-like box, and placed it near the mouth of the Johnson Street ravine for other Chinese to worship. In the absence of a proper temple, the deity was kept in that box for years. One evening a Hakka resident named Ngai Sze had a dream in which the deity told him to build a temple. The following day he started a fund-raising campaign for the construction of such a temple. This account of the temple's origin remains a shadowy legend with no factual basis.

A search of archival materials revealed that the Hakka people in Victoria probably succeeded in pooling enough money in 1875 to rent a small house at the corner of Government and Fisgard streets, which they used as Tam Kung Temple. A local newspaper reported that the temple was dedicated on the Friday night of 21 January 1876.[4] A search of deeds in the Land Registry Office revealed that the property on which the temple was located was purchased on 22 January 1877 by Tsay Ching and Dong Sang from James Porter for $753.[5] The two buyers probably purchased the temple property on behalf of the Hakka people in Victoria. An exterior facade of Oriental style was then added to the house to make it look more like a Chinese temple (Fig. 24).

During the building boom of the early 1910s, the single-storey temple was demolished and replaced by a four-storey tenement building. The Yen Wo Society, a Hakka association formed in 1905, took possession of the property on 14 October 1911, and used the top floor as Tam Kung Temple[6] (see Fig. 74). On 11 January 1980, a fire was started by an oil lamp that ignited the overhanging silk tapestries, and the blaze did extensive damage to the shrine and ceiling.[7] With the help of Victoria MLA Gordon Hanson, museum technicians were contacted to help restore some of the irreplaceable artifacts.[8] Taking photographs inside the temple had not been permitted in the past. Without a photograph of the statuette of Tam Kung, the technicians did their best to restore it as close as possible to its original form. After the fire, Ngai consulted Tam Kung and was advised that taking photographs in the temple would be permitted. The temple is open to the public every day of the week except Monday.

As one enters the temple, one is struck by the great array of

Fig. 24.
Tam Kung Temple, c. 1877.

colourfully embroidered silk banners, fans, and canopies on both sides of the hall. They were donated by worshippers as tokens of their gratitude to Tam Kung for his blessings or for granting their requests. The wood carving of the front altar table is gilded and elaborately decorated. Vases of flowers and plates of fruit are displayed on its top. Behind the front altar table is a simpler altar table on which incense burners and candlestick holders are placed. Behind this table is the shrine housing the statuette of Tam Kung (Fig. 25). At the corner near the balcony is a wooden stand holding a drum and a cast-iron bell, which are struck twice a day. The bell, dedicated in 1887, is the oldest artifact in the temple. When struck on its rim, it gives off a deep resonant tone that reverberates throughout the temple.

Worshippers come to the temple to *qiu qian* (to divine by the lot) before Tam Kung, seeking his advice on such matters as whether to go on vacation, accept a new offer, or move to a new house, and when to set a wedding or moving date. The oracular

Fig. 25. Effigy of Tam Kung, Tam Kung Temple, Victoria.

tool is a bamboo tube that holds 103 narrow bamboo sticks called *qian*, each stick bearing a number. The ritual of *qiu qian* is that a believer, kneeling down in front of Tam Kung, continuously shakes the bamboo tube, from which one stick gradually rises above the others until it topples over and falls to the floor. The numbered stick is taken to the temple custodian, who issues a small slip of paper bearing the corresponding number; oracular verses on the paper are responses from Tam Kung. The believer must consult the oracular book called "Tian Hou Ling Qian" (the Queen of Heaven's Efficacious Oracular Sticks) for answers, and very often needs a professional *qian* decipher to explain the meaning of the verses.

Another type of *qian* allows worshippers to seek prescriptions for their indispositions. Each numbered *qian* has a corresponding numbered paper bearing a prescription of Chinese herbs. The prescription of No. 64 *qian*, for example, consists of two herbs: apricot seeds and dried lily bulbs (Fig. 26). The former is used to relieve coughing and wheezing.[9] The latter is used as an attitusive and sedative for cough and haemoptysis. According to traditional Chinese medicine, the symptoms of a deficiency in the vital essence of the lung – a dry lung – include a dry throat, unproductive cough, or expectoration of blood or

譚公仙方

第六十四方

叭噠杏仁去皮尖　擣碎称時須一錢

再加百合一錢好　潤肺消痰妙藥

Prescription of Tam Kung

Number 64

Remove the peel and the tip of the bitter Apricot seeds.

Chop them into small pieces and take out 0.26 oz of them.

Add 0.13 oz of dried lily bulbs.

Boil the two herbs in water.

The medicine is good for moistening the lung, and resolving phlegm.

Fig. 26. A prescription issued according to the number of qian.

thick, sticky phlegm that is difficult to cough up. The treatment is to administer herbs that will replenish the vital essence of this organ (moisten the lung). In addition to bitter apricot seed and lily bulb, these herbs include loquat leaf, ginkgo seed, and mulberry bark.[10] After examining the prescriptions of several *qian* of the temple, a Chinese medical doctor said that they are well-tried recipes, good for health. Hence, even a person without illness will not be harmed by taking them.[11]

Tam Kung

Tam Kung is not a widely known deity in China; he is worshipped mainly in the coastal provinces of Guangdong and Fujian in South China, and particularly in Hong Kong and Macao. There are at least three legends about Tam Kung. One claims that an orphan called Tam Siu was brought up by his grandmother in

Huiyang County in Guangdong Province.[12] During his boyhood he performed incredible feats, including herding his cows to graze on a mountain that tigers frequented. Other villagers, worrying about his safety, immediately went to the mountain to look for him. To their surprise, they found him playing with the tigers. He repeatedly performed such miracles as healing incurable diseases and calming storms at sea. In one drought season he appealed to Heaven for water. After he threw a handful of peas into the air, rain began to fall on the parched crops. When he was barely twelve years old, he was deified on a mountain slope. After his death at approximately eighty years of age, he became a patron saint of the Hakka people and of seafarers in South China. He was respectfully called Tam Kung (Kung means grandpa, gentleman, or the Duke, the first of the five orders of ancient nobility in China). At an advanced age, Tam Kung still looked like a child.

Several stores on Shanghai Street, Hong Kong, specialize in making effigies or painted images of various Chinese deities (Fig. 27). There are at least four images of Tam Kung in these stores. One shows Tam Kung as a boy, seated and holding a fly-whisk; the whisk is said to be for brushing away evils. Other images depict Tam Kung holding a bell or other objects. In the two Tam Kung temples in Hong Kong, and in the Temple of the God of Tam in Macao, the statuette of Tam Kung is a child who is elaborately dressed like a lord. These statuettes are very different from the one in Victoria; Tam Kung's appearance seems to depend on the imagination of the painter or sculptor.

According to another legend, Tam Kung's surname originated with Tam, an elderly Hakka native living in Kowloon City, Hong Kong.[13] Although he was more than sixty years old, he was still very energetic and dedicated to community work. His neighbours loved him so much that they affectionately called him Tam Kung. In 1276, the Mongolian forces crossed the Yangtze River and captured Hangzhou, the capital of the Southern Song Dynasty. The imperial fleet of junks, carrying the eight-year-old Emperor Bing and his retinue, escaped from the capital and sailed down to Kowloon City. Tam Kung immediately organized the community to provide the boy emperor and the Song royalists with provisions and accommodation. He also helped organize the defence work, and repaired the ships of the Song navy. As the Mongolian forces continued to advance on Hong Kong, the

Fig. 27. Different images of Tam Kung sold in stores in Shanghai Street, Hong Kong.

fugitive emperor and his followers left in 1278 for Yashan, a promontory near Macao. The two prominent leaders, Tam Kung and Ma Nan Bao, mobilized the community to abandon their homes and follow the fleeing emperor. At Yashan, they fought the last battle with the Mongol pursuers. In the end, both Tam Kung and Ma Nan Bao were killed, and Premier Lu Xiu Fu, carrying the boy emperor, jumped into the sea and committed suicide. Semi-official history books and local gazetteers mentioned Ma Nan Bao's patriotic deeds, but not Tam Kung's. Accordingly, the Hakka people in Hong Kong made him their patron saint and built a temple in Kowloon City to honour him. He is now worshipped not only by the Hakka people, but by fishermen and boat people (people living on sampans, boats or junks moored in inlets).

A third suggestion about Tam Kung's identity is that Tam Kung is a fictitious name that in fact represents Emperor Bing, the last emperor of the Song Dynasty.[14] After his death, the boy emperor was deified. As the Mongols were in power, he was worshipped under the fictitious name of Tam Kung. Hence, he was painted as a child, holding the handbell that "was used to instruct soldiers to stand still and be silent, and for this reason became associated with veneration and respect."[15]

The four patron saints worshipped by the boat people in Hong Kong are: a) Tam Kung; b) Tian Hou, the Queen of Heaven and also the Goddess of the Sea; c) Bei Di, the Heavenly God of the North, who is believed to possess the powers of controlling rains, floods, and waters of irrigation; and d) Guan Yin, the Goddess of Mercy, who always saves people from troubles on land and at sea. Although effigies of Tian Hou, Bei Di, and Guan Yin are not in the Tam Kung Temple in Victoria, their festivals are observed here. The temple will be busy during the Bei Di Festival on the 3rd day of the 3rd lunar month; the Tian Hou Festival on the 23rd day of the 3rd month; the Tam Kung Festival on the 8th day of the 4th month; and the Guan Yin Festivals on the 19th day of the 2nd, 6th, and 9th months.

The Palace of Sages

Another important "joss house" in Chinatown is the Palace of Sages (*Lid Shing Kung*) on the second floor of the Chinese Public School at 636 Fisgard Street. The Palace of Sages is a large, gilded shrine which houses statuettes of five sages: Zhao Yuan Tan (the God of Wealth), Hua Tuo (the God of Medicine), Tian Hou (the Queen of Heaven), Kwan Yu (the God of the Military), and Confucius, China's greatest philosopher (Fig. 28).[16] These deities are worshipped by the common people in China, particularly the natives of South China.

The shrine was originally installed on the top floor of the old Chinese Consolidated Benevolent Association (CCBA) building at 556 Fisgard Street. It was frequented not only by local Chinese residents, but also by Chinese from other parts of British Columbia. Next to the Palace of Sages was the Chinese Free School. In the old days, all pupils had to assemble in front of the shrine and pay respect to the five sages before starting their classes.

The Palace of Sages fell into neglect after the 1950s. It continued to deteriorate until Jack Lee, then-president of the CCBA, decided to preserve the shrine and other artifacts, taking

Fig. 28. The Palace of Sages.

them from the old association building to the assembly hall of the Chinese Public School. On 22 May 1966 the shrine was rededicated.[17] Today the Palace of Sages is no longer a "joss house," but a showpiece of the association's rich heritage.

The Five Sages

The tall black statuette on the high altar table is Confucius (551-479 B.C.), the most honoured sage in China. He was and is still revered among the Chinese as their Supreme Sage and Foremost Teacher. His texts include the *Five Classics* and the *Four Books*. He is said to have written the *Spring and Autumn Annals*, and edited the *Classic of Poetry*, the *Classic of History*, the *Classic of Changes*, and the *Classic of Ceremonials*. This group of ancient texts is known as the *Five Classics*. After his death, his disciples assembled all of their notes and journals on his sayings and activities into a volume called the *Analects of Confucius*. During the Song Dynasty (A.D. 960-1279), Confucian scholars assembled the *Analects*, the *Mencius*, the *Great Learning*, and the *Doctrine of Mean*, naming this collection the *Four Books*. For centuries the *Four Books* and the *Five Classics* served as the syllabus for education in China. Before the Republic of China was established in 1912, the *Four Books* was used at

Fig. 29. Spirit tablets of five sages.

the primary level and the *Five Classics* at the secondary level by Chinese pupils studying at the Chinese Free School in Victoria.

In front of the shrine are ornate tablets of the five sages (Fig. 29). According to a traditional Chinese belief, a person has three souls. After death, one soul goes to the nether world to receive rewards or punishments for deeds done in the upper world. The person is then reincarnated, either as a person, a god, or an animal, according to his or her merit. The second soul goes to the grave, and the third into the spirit tablet prepared for it, where it receives the worship of descendants. Hence, it was and still is the Chinese custom to erect a spirit tablet to the dead.

Statuettes of four sages are placed inside the shrine. (The statuette of Confucius was lost, and a replacement is now put on the altar table). The black-visaged, heavily bearded statuette seated at the front is Zhao Yuan Tan[18] (Fig. 30). According to one legend, he was called Zhao Gong Ming.[19] During the Qin Dynasty (255–206 B.C.) he attained immortality at Zhong Nan Mountain, and the title of General Zhengyi Yuantan was conferred on him by the Emperor of Heaven. He was given the responsibility of sweeping out plagues, protecting people from illness, mediating disputes, and granting profits. According to another legend, Zhao Yuan Tan was formerly a member of the

Fig. 30. Effigies of four sages.

royal family of the Kingdom of Zhou during the Period of the Warring States (475-221 B.C.). After his state was conquered by the Kingdom of Qin, his family fled to Sichuan Province where, engaged in salt extraction, metal mining, and the transportation business, they soon became very rich. In spite of his wealth, Zhao Yuan Tan led a virtuous life, and was later idolized by merchants as the Lord of Wealth, becoming their patron saint.

Seated behind the God of Wealth are, from left to right, the statuettes of Hua Tuo, Kwan Yu, and Tian Hou. Hua Tuo is a historical personage, living in the Dynasty of East Han (A.D. 25-220).[20] Considered a miraculous physician by his contemporaries, he was very knowledgeable about Chinese herbs, and good at acupuncture and surgical cures for ailments. His acupuncture treatment always cured the constant headaches of Premier Cao Cao; hence, the Premier kept him by his side. Being a dedicated scholar, Hua Tuo was always ashamed of having practised medicine for money, and yearned to travel throughout the country to continue his research on herbs and treatment methods. He eventually left the Premier for his home village on the pretext that his wife was ill, and did not return even upon the Premier's summons. The Premier was so furious that he arrested Hua Tuo, imprisoned him, and tortured him to death. Before he died, Hua Tuo gave his handwritten notes on medicine to the prison guard, asking him to keep them, use them to save more lives, and pass them on to future generations. Fearing the Premier's punishment, the guard refused to accept the notes. Thereupon Hua Tuo burnt them, and his lifetime of medical knowledge was lost. After his death, he was deified as the God of Medicine, patron saint of doctors and saviour of the sick and incurable.

The red-visaged, long-bearded statuette seated in the centre of the back row is Kwan Yu.[21] He is also a historical personage, living in the Period of Three Kingdoms (A.D.220–280). Known to be brave, loyal, chivalrous, and righteous, he was not only a supreme general, but also a scholar of no mean attainments. Legend has it that he, Lau Bei, and Chang Fei vowed blood-brotherhood in Chang Fei's peach garden. The "Three Heroes' Oath in the Peach Garden" is a commonly performed episode in Chinese operas. After his death, Kwan Yu was idolized as a Saint of Courage and Righteousness because of his unmatched bravery and extreme loyalty to his blood-sworn brothers. Like the Western hero St. George, Kwan Yu stands for courage, chivalry, loyalty, and honesty. After the twelfth century, posthumous titles were conferred on him by several emperors. Emperor Hui Zong (A.D. 1101–1125) of the Song Dynasty, for example, conferred on him the title *Wu An Wang* (the King of Military Pacification). Emperor Wan Li (A.D. 1573–1619) of the Ming Dynasty bestowed on him the title *Zhong Yi Da Di* (the Supreme God of Loyalty and Righteousness). Since then Kwan Yu has been worshipped as *Kwan Di* (the Kwan God) or *Wu Di* (the God of the Military). Later, Emperor Qian Long (A.D. 1736–1795) of the Qing Dynasty added the title *Fu Mo Da Di* (the God of Subduing Demons). In 1914, the government of the Republic of China decreed that Kwan Yu and Yue Fei, a general of the Dynasty of Southern Song (A.D. 1127–1279), be worshipped together in the Temple of the Military.

The last sage of the Palace of Sages is Tian Hou. Legend has it that she was the sixth daughter of Lin Yuan, living in Fu Tian County, Fujian Province, during the Song Dynasty (A.D. 960–1127).[22] When she was born, a heavenly light shone, and the air was filled with a fragrant sweet smell. When she was a child, she could cross the sea on a rattan mattress and rest on the clouds, drifting from one island to another. The local natives called her "the daughter of the dragon." Once, when her brothers were at sea on a business trip and their ship was caught in a fierce storm, she sent forth her spirit and brought the ship back to safety. After she attained immortality, she was frequently seen in a red gown, flying over the seas to save seafarers from danger, and performing miracles from the Song Dynasty to the Yuan Dynasty (A.D. 1271–1368). Emperor Kang Xi (A.D. 1662–1723) of the Qing Dynasty conferred on her the title "Tian Fei" (Imperial Concubine of Heaven), and later honoured her as "Tian Hou" (Queen of Heaven). Like Tam Kung, she is worshipped by fishermen, sailors, and boat people, but she heads other protectors of the sea because of her high status.

Summary

Some Western people have said that the Chinese are not religious, only superstitious. But visitors in Florence and Rome see many statues of various saints, as well as images and church carvings. The worship of these is similar to the worship of the Chinese "josses." The only differences are the objects and methods of worship. Revering all divinities and spirits, the Chinese do not have one god who demands their sole devotion. Their religion is an intermixture of Taoism, Buddhism, Confucianism, folk belief, and the worship of ancestors, of heaven and earth, and of a host of gods and spirits. Offerings of food and wine in temples or at graves are tokens of respect and love. Ignorance of Chinese beliefs and customs may breed contempt. An old-timer recalled that during a Qing Ming Festival, members of a clan association laid out a roasted pig, steamed chickens, barbecued ducks, and fruit on a Chinese grave. A Caucasian lady who had placed a bundle of flowers on her husband's grave next to the Chinese one looked at the Chinese food and was much amused. She could not help asking a Chinese worshipper, "When do you expect your ancestor will eat all this food?" The reply was, "At the same time when your husband comes up to smell your flowers. If he is hungry, he is welcome to come over and have a bite." This even response may show the cultural gap between the two worshippers. An alternate reply, however, might have been, “It is an ancient Chinese custom to use food instead of flowers to show our love, reverence, and care for the dead. For many hundreds of years in China, famine and hunger were common. Because the Chinese believed that the soul of a person still existed after death, they expressed their care for the dead by feeding them well.” This reply is probably a better attempt to narrow the gap between two cultures.

«8» *Symbolism of Sidewalks and the Gate*

The street beautification and Chinese gateway projects greatly altered the streetscape of Chinatown after 1980. The first project was an extension of the established Old Town Beautification Program.[1] Initially, it concentrated on the 500 block of Fisgard Street, and the intersection of Fisgard and Government streets. All overhead wiring was placed underground, then the sidewalks were resurfaced and widened to accommodate rows of pine and cherry trees. The pavement at the northwestern and southwestern corners of Fisgard and Government streets was broadened for the installation of a Chinese Gate and a pair of stone lions. In order to understand the sidewalk symbols, it is necessary to have some knowledge of Chinese writing styles.

The Sidewalk Symbols

There are seven major styles of writing a Chinese character: the Seal Character, Ancient Official, Clerical, Running Hand, Grass, Printer's, and Artistic styles. The Chinese character *Shou* (meaning longevity), for example, may be written in any one of these styles (Fig. 31). The Seal Character, Ancient Official, and Artistic writing styles are commonly used in Chinese architecture

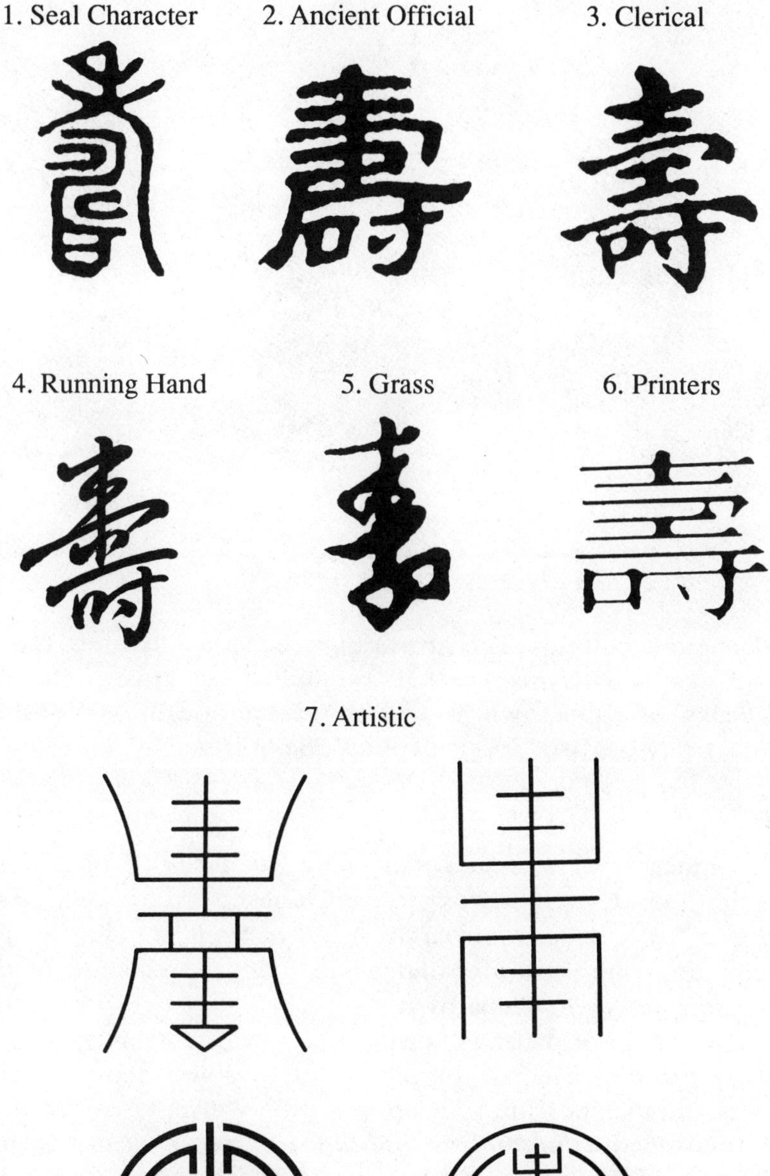

Fig. 31. The Chinese character "Shou," written in seven styles.

Fig. 32. "Shou" character on sidewalks.

as decorative patterns. The Artistic style consists of a great variety of shapes and forms created by individual artists. On the sidewalks of Chinatown, a system of interlocking red bricks delineates two artistic forms of *Shou* (Fig. 32).

Origins of Paifang

The Chinese call a freestanding gateway *paifang* or *pailou*, which loosely translates as "Chinese arch," although architecturally it is not an arch. A better understanding of the origins and functions of paifang will help appreciation of the Chinese gateway in Chinatown.

The origin of paifang is disputable. One theory suggests that paifang can be traced to the use of totem poles in ancient clan society. In ancient China, an upright pole with a cross-bar at its top was called a *huabiao* or *huabiaozhu*, meaning ornamental pillar (Fig. 33). It was erected as a locational sign for a clan settlement, tomb site, or entrance to a bridge.[2] In Beijing, for example, a pair of very tall huabiao were prominently erected in front of the Tiananmen to function as a locational mark for the entrance to the Imperial Palace. When two uprights are connected by one straight cross-piece at their top ends, they become a portal, or a paifang (Fig. 34). *Pai* means "a sign-board

Fig. 33
A huabiao.

or a placard," and *fang* means "a ward, or a subdivision of a city." Thus paifang means "a sign-board erected in a neighbourhood." Like a huabiao, it functions as a locational sign. A paifang, however, might also be elaborately built as a symbolic entrance to a temple or an imperial tomb. A series of paifang marking the entrance to the Circular Mound of the Temple of Heaven in Beijing consists of lintels across several huabiao. A *pailou* is more elaborately and massively constructed. *Lou* means "a multi-storey building"; hence, a pailou usually has roofs supported by clusters of cantilevered brackets, and looks like a storeyed building (Fig. 35). A pailou may sometimes be called a paifang, although the latter usually refers to a simpler gate.

Another theory on the origin of paifang suggests that it can be traced to the burial mound of Buddha in India, and the introduction of Buddhism to China. After Buddha died, his remains were covered by a stupa, a dome-shaped mound of

Fig. 34. Paifang marking the entrances to the Circular Mound of the Temple of Heaven, Beijing.

earth. Stupa I at Sanchi in Central India was surrounded by a balustrade that was divided into four quadrants with four entrances; each entrance was embellished with a torana, a lavishly carved gateway.[3] The torana was formed by two massive uprights jointed by three horizontal lintels or architraves.[4] After Buddhism was introduced to China during the Han Dynasty (206 B.C. – A.D. 220), Chinese Buddhists also began to build toranas in front of stupas. In China, a torana was called a paifang, and a stupa a pagoda. Gradually, a paifang or a pailou began to be utilized as a symbolic entrance to a temple, palace, or mausoleum.

During the Tang Dynasty (A.D. 618–907), the emperors commonly built paifang to commemorate an individual's virtue or to honour a town or city for its peace, security, and well-disposed customs. In doing so, they would encourage their subjects to be loyal and law-abiding. On the other hand, many individuals or cities also coveted a paifang from the emperor so that their deeds would be immortalised. The word *fang* sounds similar to the word *wang*, which means "to look up to or to hope for." Thus a paifang may also mean "a signboard of virtues which everyone looks up to or hopes for." In the Song Dynasty (A.D. 960–1273), the emperors erected *Zhen Jie Paifang* (Gates of the Undefiled) to commemorate

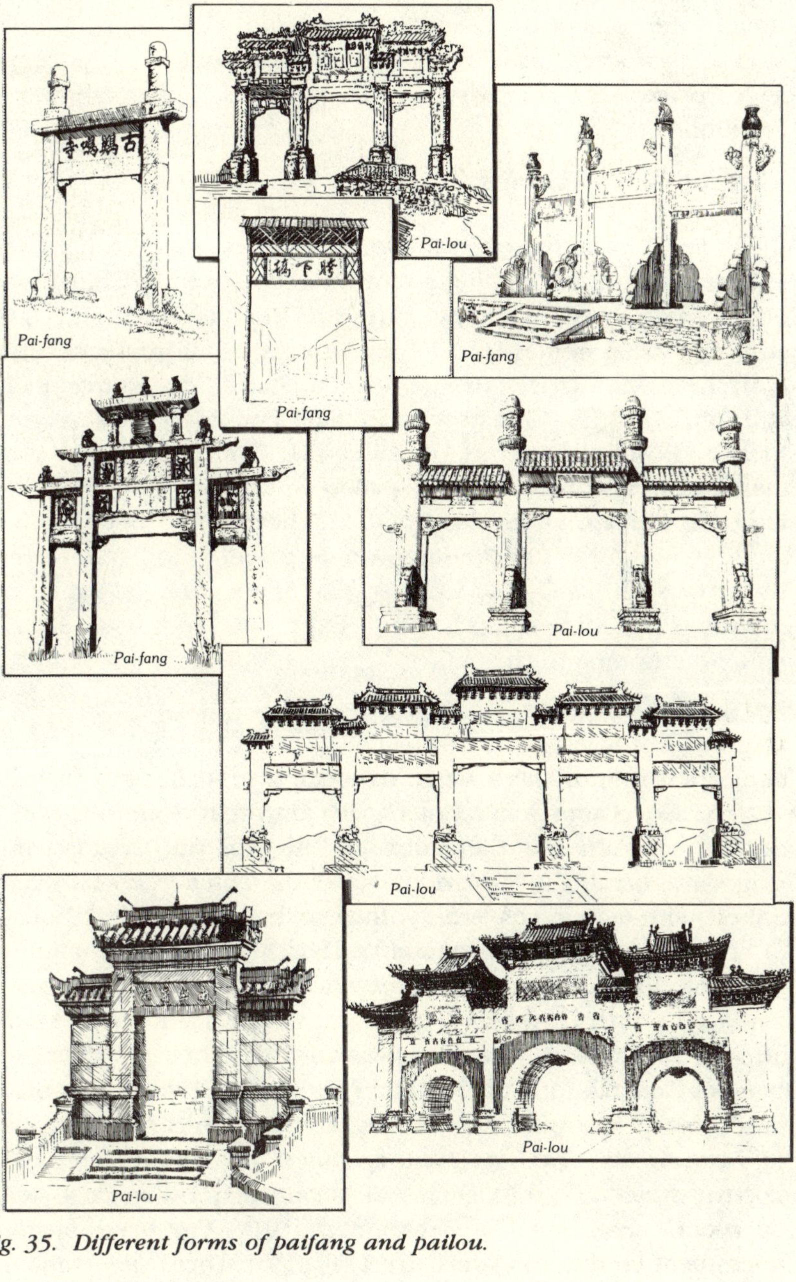

Fig. 35. Different forms of paifang and pailou.

the virtues and purity of women. The construction of paifang was more widespread throughout the Ming (1386–1644) and Qing (1644–1911) dynasties. In time, local people gradually adopted the practice of building paifang or pailou to honour visiting dignitaries, celebrate special occasions, and decorate scenic places or grand structures such as hotels and other institutions.

Pailou in North America

When the Chinese migrated to North America, they brought with them the custom of building pailou to decorate their Chinatowns. Today, freestanding Chinese gates of high architectural order occupy a prominent place in the streets of more than eleven North American cities. In the United States, decorative pailou were built in the Chinatowns of San Francisco, Los Angeles, Chicago, Boston, Portland, Philadelphia, Washington D.C., and other cities. The first Chinese pailou in Canada was erected in Victoria's Chinatown in 1981. Others have since been built in Montreal, Winnipeg, and Edmonton as proud landmarks of their Chinatowns. In 1987, the Chinese Cultural Centre in Vancouver acquired the Chinese arch from Expo '86 and used it as a symbolic entrance to the centre.[5]

Pailou in Victoria

The Chinese community in Victoria erected six paifang or pailou to welcome Governors-General of Canada on their visits to the city.[6] The first occasion was the arrival of Earl Dufferin, Canada's third Governor-General, on 16 August 1876. Three Chinese gates, covered with evergreens and adorned with lanterns, were built on Cormorant Street. On 20 September 1882, the Chinese community again built a huge gate on Store Street to welcome the Marquis of Lorne, the fourth Governor-General, and his wife, Princess Louise. The third occasion was to welcome Earl Grey, the ninth Governor-General, on 14 September 1906. A lavishly decorated Chinese gate was built across Government Street between Yates and View streets. The last time the Chinese community built a gate was to welcome the Duke of Connaught, Canada's tenth Governor-General, on 27 September 1912. The gate spanned Government Street near Yates Street (Fig. 36). These six celebrative gates were dismantled almost immediately after each occasion. They

Fig. 36. A Chinese gate on Government Street near Yates Street, 1912.

were an ephemeral form of urban art that temporarily brightened Chinatown and downtown Victoria.

The Gate of Harmonious Interest

In August 1979, the City's Chinatown Ad Hoc Committee recommended that a permanent Chinese gate be built in Chinatown as a recreation of an historic past as well as a symbol of "the spirit of cooperation and participation between our Chinese citizens and the rest of the community."[7] This concept resulted in the construction of the Gate of Harmonious Interest, which was designed by Mickey Lam, the City's urban design planner. The entire structure of the gate, 11.6 metres (38 feet) high and 16.8 metres (55 feet) wide, consists of three "arches" or openings (Fig. 37). The main arch spanning Fisgard Street has a width of 10 metres (33 feet), and two arches over the sidewalks have a span of 2.4 metres (8 feet) each. The height clearance under the main arch is 4.9 metres (16 feet), and that of the side arches is 3.4 metres (11 feet). The cladding materials, purchased from a Taiwan company, were installed by a city crew supervised by Jim Carpenter (see Fig. 40). The total cost of the gate was $130,000, of which about one-quarter was contributed

Fig. 37. The Gate of Harmonious Interest, July 1989.

by Chinese Canadians, one-quarter by non-Chinese Canadians, and the rest by the provincial government of British Columbia.[8]

The gate's name, "Tong Ji Men" (Gate of Harmonious Interest), is a constant reminder of the joint efforts by Chinese and non-Chinese citizens in Victoria to preserve the heritage of Chinatown and revive its prosperity for their mutual interest and benefit. The gate is not only a symbolic entrance to Canada's earliest Chinatown, but also a permanent monument to mark the harmony of the multicultural society that all Canadians enjoy.

The most notable features of the gate are its harmonious construction, pleasing proportions, complementary colour scheme, panel designs, and lighting effects. Its design, in form and dimension, follows the principle of symmetry, which gives the structure an orderly and distinguished look, and gives viewers a peaceful, protected feeling. The art displayed on the gate embodies the Chinese concept of the Yin-Yang equilibrium in Nature, and the harmonious unity of the dragons (Emperor and male principle) and phoenixes (Empress and female principle).

To understand the symbolism of the gate's motifs, one should have some knowledge of the Chinese people's great respect for Nature, and their philosophy about the concept of

Creation. The basic principle of Chinese cosmology is that of "unity in duality." The dualism is composed of the Yin (female) and Yang (male) elements, similar to the Adam-Eve concept. The interaction of the Yin and the Yang is thought to have given birth to everything in the Universe. Symbolically, the Yin stands for such things as the earth, moon, and phoenix, and such qualities as being feminine, subordinate, and gentle. The Yang is associated with such things as the heavens, the sun, and the dragon, and the qualities of masculinity, dominance, and vigour. The harmony of Nature is achieved through the balance and complementary workings of these two cosmic forces. This concept has been incorporated into the design of the Gate of Harmonious Interest; many of its motifs are symbolic of the balance and interaction of Yin and Yang – the harmony of Nature.

The gate's motifs also reflect the influence of a blend of Animism, Taoism, and Buddhism. In Chinese mythology, for example, the heavenly vault is divided into four quadrants, each associated with four supernatural creatures.[9] The "Azure Dragon" presides over the eastern quarter, the "Vermilion Phoenix" over the southern, the "White Tiger" over the western, and the "Black Tortoise" over the northern. The dragon represents the great celestial power, and the supreme authority. Thus Chinese emperors used it as their emblem. The dragon is also conceived as the male principle, or the yang. Ordinary people see the dragon as a beneficent creature that moves through the heavens, gathering clouds and moisture to dispense the life-giving rains. Unlike Western people, the Chinese do not see the dragon as a virgin-eating monster to be slain by heroes like St. George. On the contrary, they consider it a revered, cherished creature which brings forth blessings. The female counterpart of the dragon is the phoenix, which is said to be the "sweet dew," or "the gods' nectar," descending from heaven upon the earth. The "flagon of sweet dew" is symbolic of the sacred doctrine of Buddha; a bronze vessel is sometimes used by Buddhist priests to anoint worshippers with holy water.[10] The phoenix is an emblem of the Empress, and represents purity in the abstract.

Components of the Gate

The most significant portions of the gate are the three roofs,

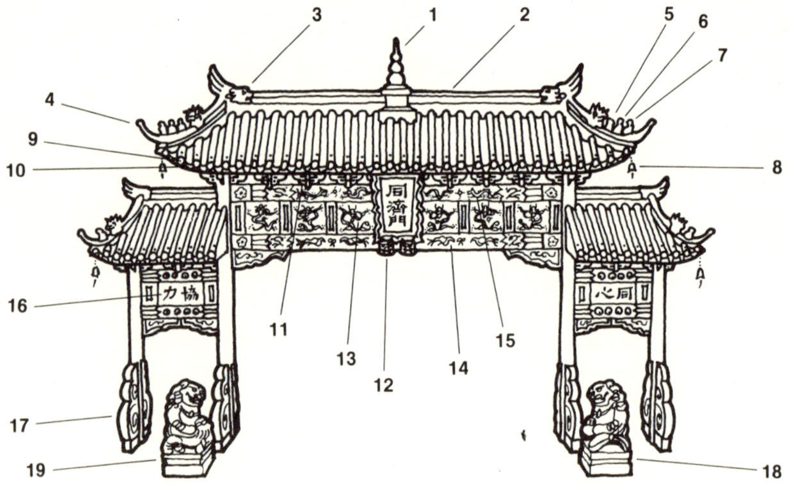

1 GOURD-SHAPED STRUCTURE
2 ROOF-RIDGE
3 CHIWEN
4 CORNER RIDGE
5 LION
6 PHOENIX
7 CHAOFENG
8 CHIME
9 CIRCULAR DISK
10 TRIANGULAR DISK
11 DOU GONG
12 BIXI
13 GOLDFOIL - GILDED DRAGON PANEL
14 GREEN PHOENIX PANEL
15 BLUE DRAGON PANEL
16 COUPLET PANEL
17 FIN
18 MALE LION
19 FEMALE LION

Fig. 38. Major components of the Gate of Harmonious Interest.

which slope down gradually and then gracefully curve up on the corners (Fig. 38). The shining glazed tiles have a tawny, yellowish colour. Yellow is an imperial colour, symbolic of supreme power in ancient China. The ridge of the central roof is surmounted by a gourd-shaped vertical structure, symbolizing the bottle-gourd carried by Li Tieguai, one of the Eight Immortals of Taoism. The gourd is used as a charm to protect against evil spirits. Two gigantic terra cotta creatures, standing up like sharks' fins, face each other from the opposite end of the roof ridge (Fig. 39). These creatures are a pair of *Chiwen*, one of the dragon's nine sons. Chiwen likes to ascend to high places and gaze open-mouthed over the landscape. Following his propensity, Chinese builders customarily place the gaping mouth of Chiwen at the end of the roof ridge, thus depicting him as performing support functions in high places. Consequently, Chiwen is nicknamed "The Beam-eater."

Fig. 39. A beam-eater.

The segmental tiles of the roof run alternately concave and convex from ridge to eaves, the convex tiles ending with circular discs, and the concave with triangular discs. Each end tile is decorated with the pattern of a plum blossom, which is an emblem of winter. The plum blossom was chosen by the Nationalist Government in Taiwan as a national flower because of its five petals, representing China's five major ethnic groups, and Dr. Sun Yat-sen's "Constitution of Five Powers."[11]

The three small terra cotta creatures on the corner ridge of the roof, from top to the bottom, are the lion, phoenix, and *Chaofeng* (Fig. 40). The Chinese consider the lion the king of all beasts; his roaring dispels phantoms. The phoenix, a supernatural bird, is believed to be the essence of water and rain, conferring blessings on the earth. *Chaofeng*, another offspring of the dragon, likes to perch on high cliffs to court dangers. Thus this daredevil is usually placed on the precipitous end of the corner ridge so that he feels more at home. This row of animals is believed to ward off evil spirits and protect against fire. Metal chimes, symbolic of the sacred bells of the Buddhists or Taoists, are hung at eave corners. They ring when the wind blows, and their sound is believed to disperse evil spirits.

The roofs of the gate are visually supported by *Dou Gong*,

Fig. 40. Three creatures astriding on the corner ridge of the roof.

which are wooden clusters of cantilevered brackets. A set of *Dou Gong* is an assemblage of a number of *Dou* (blocks) and *Gong* (arms). Its function is to transfer the load from the horizontal member above to the vertical member below. Underneath the central roof is the name plate for the gate, bearing the three Chinese characters "Tong Ji Men." The name plate, bordered with decorative wood trim, is supported by a pair of *Bixi*, another son of the dragon. *Bixi* looks similar to a tortoise, and likes to carry heavy weights. The name plate is flanked by square panels decorated with goldfoil gilded dragons. Overlying and underlying the square panels are wooden panels of dragons and phoenixes. The blue dragon panels are symbolic of the blue sky (the male principle), and the green phoenix panels represent the verdant earth (the female principle). The blue and green panels and the pattern of auspicious colourful clouds on a green background reinforce the concept of "unity in duality" – heaven and earth, dragon and phoenix, and yin and yang.

Underneath the side roofs of the gate are the couplet panels. On the eastern front of the gate facing Government Street, the

Fig. 41.
A couplet panel, bearing two Chinese characters which mean "with one heart."

first line of verse, reading from right to left, is "Tongxin Xieli," meaning "To Work Together with One Heart" (Fig. 41). On the western front facing Store Street is the second line, which reads "Hezhong Gongji" (To Help Each Other to Achieve Harmony).

Unusually high fins (three metres, or ten feet) protect the four red columns of the gate against possible vandalism or damage by motor accidents. A brass plaque, dedicated to donors of $100 or more, is mounted on the southern main column. Another plaque, set on the sidewalk between the two southern columns, indicates the location of a time capsule, which is stored in a waterproof concrete underground vault. The capsule, a vacuum cylinder twenty-five centimetres (ten inches) in diameter, contains the C-FAX 1070 Donors' Name Roll; names of all the donors; the last issues of the two local newspapers (the *Victoria Times*, Saturday 30 October 1980, and the *Daily Colonist*, Sunday 31 October 1980); an album of photos of people involved in the construction of the gate; a copy of the Chinatown Gateway

Fig. 42.
One of the pair of stone lions at the Gate of Harmonious Interest.

Committee Report, 1980; and a copy of David Lai's 1981 book *The Gate of Harmonious Interest: From Concept to Reality* and other documents about the gateway project. The time capsule will be opened on 15 November 2081. The gate, installed with a concealed electrical and sound system, is lit up every night.

The pair of stone lions placed in front of the gate was donated to Victoria by the City of Suzhou, her sister city in Jiangsu Province, China. The lions were modelled after the sculptured lions in Tiger Hills in the western suburb of Suzhou. The lion is not native to China. One legend says it was a gift from the emperor of Parthia (now Iran) to Emperor Zhang Di of the East Han dynasty during his reign (A.D. 75–88).[12] According to another legend, the lion was introduced to China in connection with Buddhism. As a Buddhist symbol of the Guardian of the Law, it watches over the entrance of a temple, palace, or tomb. Hence, a pair of lions is often placed in front of a paifang, a symbolic entrance. The male lion, holding an orb with a ribbon in his forepaws, is on the left-hand side (the northern side), and the female lion, breast-feeding her cub, is placed on the right-hand side (the southern side) of the gate (Fig. 42). This arrangement follows the traditional Chinese custom of having the yang element on the left side of an object, and the yin element on the right.

Summary

When the gate was dedicated on 15 November 1981, Alderman Robert H. Wright, Chairman of the Chinatown Ad Hoc Committee, said, "It is fitting that Canada's first permanent traditional Chinese arch has been built to celebrate Canada's earliest Chinatown . . . Chinatown is an integral part of downtown Victoria to which it adds its own distinctive atmosphere to the variety, vitality, and interest of a vibrant city centre. This permanent symbol represents the determination of all citizens to ensure its recognition and its continued prosperity."[13] Thus, the Gate of Harmonious Interest is not only an urban art form and a tourist attraction, but also a permanent monument to the Chinese heritage in the city, and a way of preserving and recreating the historic past of Victoria's Chinatown.

«9» *Symbolism of Building Facades*

Consider a group of tourists strolling toward a certain district of a city. Suddenly, a girl exclaims, "Chinatown is in front of us." Does she immediately see that the area in front of her is a Chinatown? Or does she see a Chinatown only after something else has taken place? The fact is, she first sees light in some configuration, and then becomes aware of the visual components that make up a specific pattern. She soon goes on to interpret the pattern, recognizing it as some kind of ethnic district. In this case, it is called a Chinatown. This direct observation of a Chinatown through the eyes is an experience of visual perception. Hence, Chinatown is a perceptual area. The perception is formed partly by seeing and partly by the mind, which operates by knowledge and experience.

The facades of Chinatown structures constitute the most striking visual component of place character. Although a homogeneous style of Chinatown architecture has never developed, Chinatown buildings usually contain structural components and decorative details rarely or never found on other downtown buildings. The common structural and decorative elements of Chinatown buildings include: (1) a

Fig. 43.
A parapet wall and a recessed balcony.

flagpole on which a Chinese flag is sometimes flown; (2) a parapet wall bearing an inscription and/or the date of construction of the building (Fig. 43); (3) sloping tiled roofs; (4) upturned eaves and roof corners (Fig. 44); (5) extended eaves over balconies; (6) decorative balustrades and ornamental fretwork; (7) smooth or carved columns topped with *Dou Gong*, a cantilevered cluster of beams; (8) a recessed or projecting balcony in the front and/or at the back of a building; (9) cheater storeys; (10) moon-shaped doors and/or windows overlain with ornate lattice work; (11) horizontal and vertical signboards bearing Chinese characters; (12) a colour scheme of gold, red, green, yellow, and other brilliant colours; (13) animal motifs of dragons, phoenixes, lions, and so on; (14) plant motifs of pine, bamboo, plum, and the like; (15) other decorative motifs such as pagodas, lanterns, bowls, and chopsticks; and (16) Chinese fittings such as *Baqua* (the Eight Trigrams), Chinese lanterns, banners, and bunting.[1] The origin, function, and symbolism of some of these elements are described in this chapter.

Recessed or Projecting Balconies

Recessed or projecting balconies dominate the upper storeys of Chinatown buildings. The recessed balcony may be a duplication of practices in Hong Kong, Macao, Guangzhou (Canton), and other cities in South China, where the facade of a building is set back at each level, and the facade plane is met by a balcony (Fig. 45). A recessed balcony is a common architectural form in subtropical China, for several reasons. First, it helps keep building interiors cool in the hot summer and warm in the cold winter. Second, it is an open space in which children can play and adults can sit down together to chat and relax after work. Third, it provides a covered place in which residents can dry their clothing on rainy days. Fourth, it functions as a courtyard in which a household can set up a temporary alter to worship the heaven during the Chinese New Year and other religious or folk festivals. Lastly, rich and influential officials in traditional China usually liked to have buildings with balconies so that they could look down upon the common people below, and the common people could look up to them. Hence, a balcony might be a symbol of power and superiority. Most Chinese tong buildings in Victoria's Chinatown have recessed balconies. A tong building that does not, usually has a projected iron balcony bolted onto the facade; the balcony is very often as wide as a fire escape. In most cases, an iron balcony was built to replace a projected wooden balcony that once extended over the sidewalk. A recessed or projected balcony is particularly useful when there is a street parade, or when the interior assembly hall of a tong is too crowded during a festival celebration.

Cheater Storey

A "cheater storey," similar to a low-ceiling mezzanine, is an extra floor that is created within a floor. It is another common feature in Chinatown buildings. It is so named because in the early days in British Columbia taxes were assessed on the height of a building, not on its total floor area. Thus an owner could "cheat," or avoid a higher building assessment rate, by creating an

Fig. 44.
Tiled roofs with upturned eaves and corners.

intermediate floor between the ground floor and the second floor. This extra floor was not assessed for taxation.

Incurved Roofs

A tiled roof with upturned eaves and corners is one of the most elegant features of Chinese architecture. It also occupies a primary position in a Chinatown building, giving it an aesthetic depth and graceful curve. The origin of the incurved roof is disputed. According to the tent hypothesis, a curved roof is a conscious imitation of the natural sweep of the tents in which ancient Chinese nomads lived. When they became sedentary agriculturalists, they built houses with incurved roofs to remind them of their nomadic dwellings. Their tent was peaked, and sagged from the ridge pole to corner props. Hence the roofs of their houses, concave on the upper side, are also peaked, and eaves tilt skyward.[2]

According to the horn hypothesis, animal horns were

closely associated with worship and sacrifice. The Moon God in the Middle East, for example, was represented by the horns of a heifer, and horns were seen protruding from the sides of certain shrines of the Qiang tribe and from some Tibetan houses.[3] This primitive reverence for horns has continued to show its influence on the Chinese in the form of talismans or ornaments. This may explain the curves of Chinese temples and houses.

Actually, a steep incurved roof may be built to withstand windstorm stresses. The concave sweep from the ridgepole to the eaves calls for a series of short rafters rather than long, straight ones, which increases the flexibility of the roof frame.[4] During a heavy rainstorm, the steep incline of the roof provides efficient drainage for rainwater, while the gentle upward slope at the bottom throws the water some distance out from the wall of the house. Furthermore, an oncoming strong wind will be deflected upward by a steep, concave roof. Over a straight, gently sloping roof, a strong wind flowing over the ridge may create a vacuum underneath, and peel off the tiles. The *Dou Gong* (clusters of cantilevered brackets) help to damp earthquake oscillations, and also uniformly distribute the weight of the wide eaves, making those parts of the structure less vulnerable. The larger the roofs, the more they seem to be disengaged from the supporting framework. In many instances, the roofs crown the buildings rather than covering them.[5] Curved eaves and roof corners may also have other advantages. On a sunny day, for example, they enable more sunlight to get into the house, and facilitate ventilation. All in all, the Chinese incurved roof may be the result of a combination of religious, aesthetical, and rational considerations.

Colour Scheme

Chinese decorative art is characterized by the use of brilliant colours and striking or grotesque outlines. Red, yellow, gold, and "qing" are the most favoured colours for the decorative details of Chinatown motifs. To the Chinese, red means joy, festivity, and luck; gold symbolizes wealth, glory, and prosperity. Hence, both red and gold are employed for many decorative details of restaurants and gift shops in Chinatown, and for all festive occasions.

Yellow, the ochre colour of the silt in the Yellow River, was

Fig. 45. Recessed balcony in tenement buildings, Guangzhou, China.

considered a symbol of mother earth by the ancient Chinese, and used as the imperial colour by emperors. It is a spiritual colour to Buddhist monks, whose saffron robes vary in shade from yellow to orange to red. Red is considered a yang element, and yellow a yin. A palace with red walls and yellow roofs is symbolic of the union of Heaven and Earth.

"Qing" refers to blue or green, because ancient Chinese probably made no distinction between the shades of blue. They called them "Qing tian" (Blue sky) or "Qing cao" (Green grass). "Qing" is associated with the wood element, and symbolizes growth, harmony, and peace. Green tiles are used as an emblem of the bounty of Nature.

White, black, and blue are seldom used in ornamentation because they are mourning colours, used at funerals. Modern Chinese, however, influenced by Western culture, now hold white in the same regard Westerners do, associating it with purity, sacredness, and innocence.

Animistic Motifs

The motifs of Chinatown buildings are strongly animistic. The four great mythical animals in China are the dragon, phoenix, unicorn, and tortoise. Although they are employed in abundance in motifs, no one has ever seen a real dragon, phoenix, or unicorn. Do they exist? According to one hypothesis, different tribes in ancient China probably used different animals, such as big snakes, tigers, or eagles, as tribal symbols or totems. A tribe was sometimes known by the name of its totem, which members considered holy and prayed to. During the Han Dynasty, a gigantic beast began to appear in art motifs, combining the features of other animals and birds – a doe's horn, an ox's ear, a carp's plate-like scales, an eagle's claw, a tiger's paw, and a snake's body – with a jagged spine and long tail. This powerful beast was then called a dragon. Gradually, the Chinese came to consider the dragon their totem, calling themselves the "descendants of the dragon," and China "the homeland of the dragon." With an all-pervading force, the dragon symbolizes the national spirit of China, and the character of its people. It was and still is believed to be a carrier of riches and harmony, exerting its beneficent influence on earth. Hence, it is commonly used as a motif in Chinatown, symbolizing prosperity and supremacy.

Where there is a dragon, a phoenix is seldom far away. Like the dragon, this supernatural bird is adorned with everything that is beautiful among birds and animals. It is said to resemble a wild swan in the fore and a unicorn behind, with a flare of feathers, a swallow's throat, a fowl's bill, a snake's neck, a fish's tail, a crane's forehead, and a mandarin duck's crown.[6] The phoenix is said to appear in times of peace and prosperity, and is another common motif in Chinatown.

The unicorn, or *Qilin*, is said to resemble a large stag in general form, with a musk deer's body, an ox's tail, a wolf's forehead, a horse's hoofs, and colourful skin.[7] It is gentle and benevolent to all living creatures. Its appearance always foretells some splendid or propitious event, such as the crowning of a benevolent monarch or the birth of a sage. An auspicious animal, the unicorn is used as a motif symbolizing good omens.

The lion, an emblem of valour and authority, is not indigenous to China, although it has been used symbolically in Chinese art since the first century A.D. Many of the early artists had probably not seen a real lion, so they portrayed it in different forms and shapes which bore little resemblance to the real animal. A female lion, for example, is also given the male lion's heavy, curly mane. Sculptured lions sometimes appear perched on corner ridges of roofs, or at the tops of balustrades.

Many other animals are employed for decorative purposes. The crane, for example, one of the emblems of longevity, is believed to be a courier of the immortal. Some animals are used in motifs because of the association of homophones with ideas. For example, the word "bat" and the word "blessing" are pronounced "fu" in both Cantonese and Mandarin. Hence, a motif *Wu Fu* (five bats) symbolizes the five blessings: longevity, wealth, healthiness, virtue, and natural death. Similarly, both the word "fish" and "superfluity" are pronounced "yu"; hence, a fish is emblematic of abundance and surplus. The deer is believed to live to a very great age, and the word "deer" is pronounced "lu," as is the word "emolument." The deer therefore symbolizes longevity as well as wealth.

Floral Motifs

Floral designs are commonly used in Chinatown motifs. Pine, bamboo, and plum trees (*Armeniaca mume*) are known as the "three soul mates of chilly winter." Staying green in winter, they are emblems of longevity and old age. The ancient Chinese believed that the peach trees of the gods in heaven blossomed once every three thousand years, their fruit taking another three thousand years to ripen. Thus, a peach tree, or a peach, is also a symbol of longevity and immortality,

The Chinese use four flowers to represent the seasons: the peony symbolizes spring; the lotus, summer; the chrysanthemum, autumn; and the plum, winter. Designs of these flowers are commonly employed in architecture, paintings, and embroidery. The peony, an emblem of love, affection, and feminine beauty, is honoured by the Chinese with the titles "King of Flowers" and "Flowers of Riches and Honours." Lotus is regarded as a sacred flower by both Buddhists and Taoists. It grows out of a muddy pond, but remains clean, just as Buddha was born into the world but lived above the world. Hence, Buddha is usually represented seated on the lotus, which symbolizes purity and perfection. The flower is also esteemed by the Taoists because He Xiangu, one of the Eight Immortals of Taoism, carries the lotus in her hand or poses on a floating lotus petal. Chrysanthemum, a symbol of joviality, is associated with leisure and retirement. Many retired officials in ancient China enjoyed cultivating chrysanthemum, which can been grown in many varieties in China. The Chinese call the plum "Leader of Flowers" because the tree blossoms first in the cold winter.

Several other flowers have been used as decorative motifs. The orchid, for example, symbolizes love and beauty. Ancient Chinese named plum, orchid, chrysanthemum, and bamboo the "Si Junzi" (the Four Perfect Gentlemen) among flowers because of their exquisite and refined characteristics. Hence, they are commonly grouped together in a design.

Many other animals, plants, and religious objects like pagodas and gourds are used in decorative designs. They are so numerous that it is beyond the scope of this volume to describe each one in connection with its legend or folklore. Certain objects, such as chopsticks, rice bowls, and rickshaws, are rarely or never used as decorative motifs in Chinese architecture, although they are used in some Chinatown restaurants. New symbols and motifs, such as the Great Wall and the panda, are being introduced to Chinatown architecture. All of these Chinese motifs and colours have helped develop a homogeneity in Chinatown, carrying over from building to building and knitting them together into a unique urban fabric.

« 10 » Heritage Buildings on Pandora Avenue

Thirty-two buildings with high heritage value have been identified in Chinatown (Fig. 46 and Table 5, pg. 108). Over ninety percent of them were built before the outbreak of the First World War. A Chinatown building may occupy entirely, less, or more than one standard lot, which measures 60 feet wide and 120 feet long (Fig. 47). In the early days, it was common practice for Caucasian landowners to give long-term leases of their land, usually more than twenty years, to the Chinese, who were then obliged to pay for the construction of a building on each site. A few wealthy Chinese merchants, however, could afford to buy the land and construct their own buildings. I have coined a name for each heritage building in Chinatown for the convenience of identifying it. The name is based on the name(s) of the Chinese or non-Chinese owner(s) who built the building, or the Chinese company, family, or individuals who first leased or owned the property. The photograph of each building shows its primary profile – the facade in full frontal view, in which the building's elevation and structural and decorative components are dominant, striking the strongest silhouette to hold viewers' eyes.

Although information on who designed the buildings in

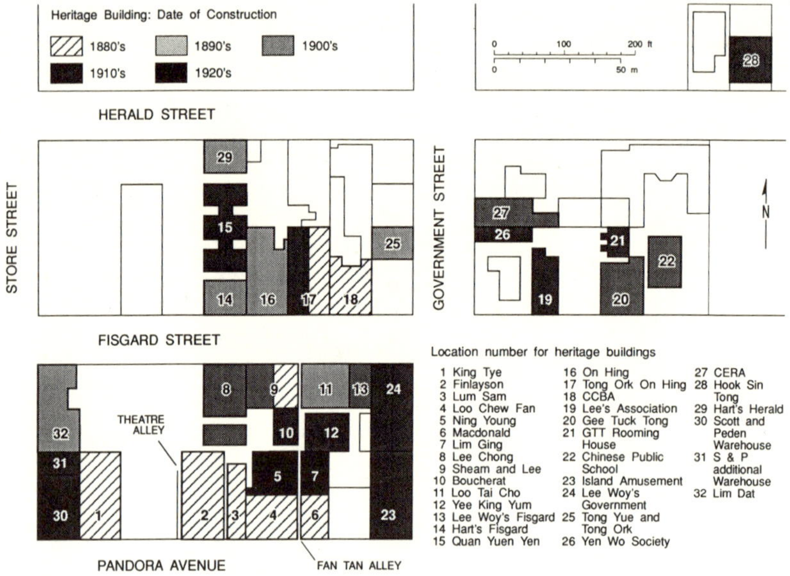

Fig. 46. Location of heritage buildings in Chinatown.

Chinatown is meagre, seven architects have been identified (Table 6, pg. 109). C. Elwood Watkins and Thomas Hooper were probably the most popular architects in Chinatown, since at least eight out of the thirty-two heritage buildings were designed by them.

Pandora Avenue between Government and Store streets is the oldest section of Chinatown. The seven heritage buildings on its northern side include:

1. King Tye Building at 512–516
2. Finlayson Building at 528–530
3. Lum Sam Building at 534
4. Loo Chew Fan Building at 536–540
5. Ning Young Building behind 536–540 (2–14 Fan Tan Alley)
6. Macdonald Building at 546–548
7. Lim Ging Building behind 546–548 (3–11 Fan Tan Alley)

1. King Tye Building, c. 1887

The King Tye Company, one of the largest Chinese import and export companies in Victoria, leased this warehouse on Lot 434 in the 1880s (Fig. 48). At its rear was the King Tye Opium Factory. In July 1901, the building was sold to Chu Lai for

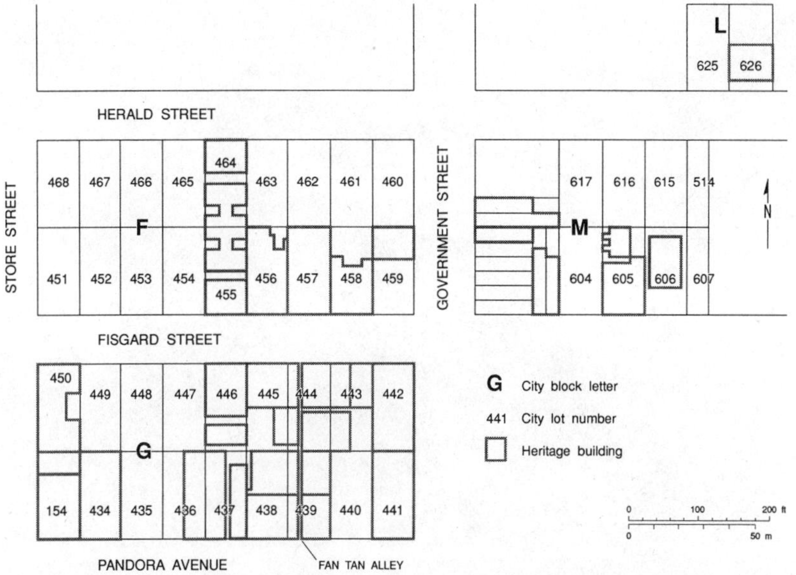

Fig. 47. City block letters and lot numbers of plots in Chinatown.

$4,000.[1] For more than two decades it was owned by Chinese, until Chu Kum Toa and Chu Sing Hor sold it in January 1927 to John A. Scott, William Peden, and John Peden, owners of Scott & Peden Ltd.[2] In 1973 the property was sold to James Richardson & Sons for $200,000.[3]

The facade of the early warehouse, reconstructed in 1913, was much altered in the 1980s by the addition of a retail office space, designed by Percy Fox.[4]

2. Finlayson Building, 1882

Roderick Finlayson built this building on E 30'of Lot 436 and W 25' of Lot 437 (Fig. 49). On 6 January 1883, it was reported in the *Victoria Daily Colonist* that "Cormorant Street, below Government, has been much improved by the erection of two large brick and stone two storey stores, one belonging to Hon. R. Finlayson."[5] In November 1912, Finlayson sold the building to Chong Hooie for $40,000.[6] For the next two decades, the building was Chinese-owned. Its last Chinese owner (of the Ying Chong Lung Co. Ltd.) lost the property in November 1931 to the City of Victoria for tax arrears.[7] In July 1942, it came back into Chinese hands when Lee Gan and Chu Sing Hor bought the

Fig. 48. The King Tye Building.

building from the City for $1,165.[8] Five years later Lee Gan sold his share to Chu Sing Hor, who after his death in 1960 willed the property to his three sons, Bing Gong, Bing Horn, and Bing Chung.[9] In 1990, section E 30' of Lot 436 (the western half of the building) was sold to the City of Victoria.

This building has a remarkably unified Italianate facade with a bracketed cornice, decorative window heads on the second floor, and arcading on the ground floor. The door located on the second storey suggests that a balcony once projected over the sidewalk. To the west of the building runs the old but extant Theatre Alley, which was the access to the Chinese Theatre.

3. Lum Sam Building, c. 1884

In 1883, Lum Sam and Look Dan leased the property on the E 35' of Lot 437 from Roderick Finlayson for twenty-five years.[10] Having raised a $3,000 mortgage, they built this building in the following year (Fig. 50). After 1909, the property changed hands several times, finally being acquired by the City of Victoria in December 1935 through tax arrears.[11] In May 1941 the City sold the property to Lee Chow for $1,015.[12] The present owners, Chu Bing Gong, Chu Bing Horn, and Chu Bing Chung, inherited it in February 1956.[13]

Fig. 49. The Finlayson Building.

The facade of this small building displays decorative brickwork and symmetrical Italianate windows. The second-storey doorway opened to a wooden balcony, which was later replaced by a cast iron balcony to accommodate the City's fire regulations in the 1890s (Fig. 51). To the western side of the building runs a passage leading to two interior courtyards and two more narrow passages, which together form an internal passageway through the three tenement buildings from Pandora Avenue to Fisgard Street.

4. Loo Chew Fan Building, c. 1884

This building was built on a site covering Lot 438 and W 20' of Lot 439 (Fig. 52). Loo Choo Sing bought the site from James Porter in May 1880, selling it eight months later to Loo Chew Fan.[14] Having raised a $3,500 mortgage, Loo built this building in 1884. By default, he lost the building to Albert Ofner, who in October 1904 sold the property to the Ning Young Yee Hing Tong.[15] The tong, formed by the Chinese from Hoy Sun (Taishan) county, was renamed in 1914 as the Hoy Sun Ning Young Benevolent Association. Retail stores now occupy the street level, and residential accommodation the second floor. The association office is located on the ground floor in the eastern part of the building.

Fig. 50.
The Lum Sam Building in the 1880s.

A closeup of the building's facade in the 1880s shows the large corner brackets in the spandrels between the posts and the balcony (Fig. 53). This particular style, resembling Gothic cusping, may have derived from debased chinoiserie designs. The original facade of the building has been much altered by the removal of the wooden balcony, the walled-up entrances and windows at the street level, and the unsympathetic addition of smaller windows and doors. In spite of this alteration, the original decorative brickwork at the cornice and the Italianate heads of the windows on the top storey can still be identified, and harmonize with those of adjacent buildings.

5. Ning Young Building, 1920

Ning Young Yee Hing Tong engaged C. Elwood Watkins to

Fig. 51.
The Lum Sam Building, 1991.

design and build this building in 1920 (see Fig. 20). It is relatively intact, except for the removal of its metal cornice, for which the angled hanger brackets still remain.[16] Like other buildings fronting Fan Tan Alley, this building once had stores on the ground floor and tenements on the upper floors.

6. Macdonald Building, c. 1885

In 1885, William J. Macdonald leased the lot on E 40' of Lot 439 to the Chinese, who then built this commercial and residential building.[17] In January 1908, it was sold to Lim Bang, Wong Yock, and Wong Tong for $10,500.[18] Having changed hands several times, it was finally acquired in December 1938 by the City of Victoria through tax arrears.[19] In January 1914, the property was bought by James Y. Lim for $1,770, and remained in Chinese ownership until the 1970s.[20]

Fig. 52. The Loo Chew Fan Building, 1991.

Fig. 53. The Loo Chew Fan Building in the 1880s.

Fig. 54. The Macdonald Building after renovation, 1989.

This Italianate building is characterized by its bracketed window hoods and cornice. The full length of double-hung windows on the second floor provided access to a wooden balcony which was later replaced by a small projecting wrought-iron one, a familiar feature of Chinatown buildings. The building was left vacant for several years in the early 1980s after its interior was demolished from the ground to the roof. It was renovated in 1988, and its original facade on the second floor was preserved (Fig. 54).

7. Lim Ging Building, 1920

Lim Ging and Lee Ward engaged C. Elwood Watkins to design this building, and built it in 1920 (see Fig. 21). The storefronts facing Fan Tan Alley continue the rhythm of brick structures down the alley. Although the interior has been completely altered, its facade facing the alley remains relatively intact.

Table 5
A List of Heritage Buildings in Chinatown

Location Number	*Name of Building*	*Address*	*Date of Construction*
		Pandora Avenue	
1	King Tye	512-516	c. 1887
2	Finlayson	528-530	1882
3	Lum Sam	534	c. 1884
4	Loo Chew Fan	536-540	c. 1884
5	Ning Young	behind 536-540 (2-14 Fan Tan Alley)	1920
6	Macdonald	546-548	c. 1885
7	Lim Ging	behind 546-548 (3-11 Fan Tan Alley)	1920
		Fisgard Street	
8	Lee Chong	533-537	1901
9	Sheam and Lee	539-545	1888/1901
10	Boucherat	behind 539-545 (16-20 Fan Tan Alley)	1912
11	Loo Tai Cho	549-555	c. 1893
12	Yee King Yum	behind 549-555 (17-25 Fan Tan Alley)	1913
13	Lee Woy's Fisgard	557-561	1908
14	Hart's Fisgard	532-534	c. 1890
15	Quan Yuen Yen	behind 532-534	1912
16	On Hing	538-544	c. 1891
17	Tong Ork On Hing	546-552	1882/1914
18	CCBA	554-562	1885
19	Lee's Association	612-614	1911
20	Gee Tuck Tong	622-626	1903
21	GTT Rooming House	behind 622-626	1913
22	Chinese Public School	636	1909
		Government Street	
23	Island Amusement	1600	1913
24	Lee Woy's Government	1618-1628	1910
25	Tong Yue & Tong Ork	1712-1714	1897
26	Yen Wo Society	1713	1912
27	CERA	1715-1717	1905
		Herald Street	
28	Hook Sin Tong	658-664	1911
29	Hart's Herald	529-539	c. 1890
		Store Street	
30	Scott & Peden Warehouse	1601-1613	1913
31	S & P Additional Warehouse	1615	1913
32	Lim Dat	1619-1627	1898

Table 6
A List of Architects of Chinatown Buildings, 1893-1920

Name of Architect	*Name of Building*	*Date of Construction*
William Ridgeway Wilson	Loo Tai Cho	1893
David C. Frame	Chinese Public School	1909
L.W. Hargreaves	Yen Wo Society	1912
Samuel Buttrey Birds	Quan Yuen Yen	1912
M.S. Farwell	Scott & Peden Warehouse	1913
Thomas Hooper	Lim Dat	1898
	Yee King Yum	1913
Thomas Hooper and C. Elwood Watkins	Lee Woy's Fisgard	1908
C. Elwood Watkins	Lee Woy's Government	1910
	Hook Sin Tong	1911
	Boucherat	1912
	Lim Gin	1920
	Ning Young	1920

« 11 » Heritage Buildings on Fisgard Street

Buildings on Fisgard Street typify Chinatown at the turn of the twentieth century. They are characterized by a mixture of residential and commercial uses, with tenements and association offices on the upper floors, stores on the ground floors, and tenements, gambling dens, or opium factories at the rears. There are eleven heritage buildings in the 500 block, and four in the 600 block.

(A) The 500 Block of Fisgard Street

8. Lee Chong Building at 533-537
9. Sheam and Lee Building at 539-545
10. Boucherat Building behind 539-545 (16-20 Fan Tan Alley)
11. Loo Tai Cho Building at 549-555
12. Yee King Yum Building behind 549-555 (17-25 Fan Tan Alley)
13. Lee Woy's Fisgard Building at 557-561
14. Hart's Fisgard Building at 532-534
15. Quan Yuen Yen Building behind 532-534
16. On Hing Building at 538-544
17. Tong Ork On Hing Building at 546-552
18. CCBA Building at 554-562

Fig. 55. The Lee Chong Building.

(B) The 600 Block of Fisgard Street

19. Lee's Association Building at 612-614
20. Gee Tuck Tong Building at 622-626
21. GTT Rooming House behind 622-626
22. Chinese Public School at 636

8. Lee Chong Building, 1901

In January 1901, Lee Chong and Lee Woy purchased the site on Lot 446 and built this commercial and residential building (Fig. 55).[1] The property was owned by Chinese until December 1933, when it was acquired by the City of Victoria through tax arrears.[2] In August 1940, Chong Louie bought the property from the City for $2,860, selling it six years later to W.N. Stoba for $8,000.[3] The property stayed in non-Chinese hands until May 1954, when it was sold for $11,000 to Chu Bing Gong, Chu Bing Horn, and Chu Bing Chung, who together also owned the Finlayson and Lum Sam buildings on Pandora Avenue.[4] The upper floor was converted into apartments. Today, the ground floor houses the Chinese Canadian Cultural Association and two shops.

During the early 1900s, there was a marked rejection of the

Victoria taste for elaborate architectural decoration, and a preference for plainer buildings utilizing the textures of brick, stone, and wood.[5] In commercial buildings, for example, brick cornices and mouldings replaced the applied tin and plaster detailing. This building shows the intrusion of this style into Chinatown, and provides a handsome contrast to the more ornate Italianate facade of its neighbours. The exterior remains remarkably intact, including the wrought-iron balconies over the wooden storefronts.[6] An admirably proportioned arcade of segmental windows and doors gives access to the balconies. The central embrasure on the second storey is glazed with coloured glass and set in a lattice, which could have been meant as a fretwork pattern. Behind the door is a narrow passage leading to an interior courtyard and a small brick tenement building, through which an internal passageway leads to another courtyard and the alley between the Lum Sam and Finlayson buildings on Pandora Avenue.

9. Sheam and Lee Building, 1888 and 1901

In 1881, Loo Chew Fan and Loo Chuck Fan purchased Lot 445 from Roderick Finlayson for $1,800 and the western twenty feet of Lot 444 from William J. Macdonald for $500.[7] The site was sold in June 1887 to Sheam Tip and Low Yan San, who in the following year built the first portion of the building, the eastern two bays next to Fan Tan Alley (Fig. 56).[8] Sheam Tip and Low Yan San sold the property in April 1890 to Laurent Guichon for $13,050, who sold it two months later to Jules Boucherat for $17,750.[9] Boucherat died in May 1900, leaving the property to Marie Boucherat.[10] In the following year, Lee Mong Kow, a government interpreter and a prominent Chinese community leader, leased the property and added the second portion of the building, the two western bays facing Fisgard Street. The second floor housed tenements, and the ground floor retail spaces. In the 1900s, Shon Yuen Opium Factory was established in the rear of the building. In August 1949, George Joe, Chow Shoon Wing, Chu Tait Yen, and Joe Wah pooled their resources to purchase the building from Anthony C. Coit for $25,000.[11] In November 1951, they formed the Kin Wah Co Ltd., which became the registered owner of the property.

This building is ornamented with an Italianate cornice, and a

Fig. 56. The Sheam and Lee Building.

Fig. 57. The storefront of 545 Fisgard in the 1900s.

regular arched window pattern on the second floor. A wrought-iron balcony, a typical feature of Chinatown buildings, once extended the length of the building, but in 1955 the western section of the balcony was removed and a steel fire escape added. The storefronts have been much altered (Fig. 57). The western section was framed in wood and heavily glazed, whereas the eastern section still retains its segmental-headed masonry openings.

10. Boucherat Building, 1912

This brick building, designed by C. Elwood Watkins, was built behind the Sheam and Lee Building; both buildings were owned by Marie Boucherat. The Boucherat Building was leased to the Chinese until August 1949, when it was sold to a group of Chinese: George Joe, Chow Shoon Wing, Chu Tait Yen, and Joe Wah.

Continuing the line of other brick structures fronting Fan Tan Alley, the facade of the Boucherat Building features shallow arched second-floor windows. Its brick cornice is an excellent example of a corbelled treatment.[12] The building is separated from Ning Young building by a narrow alley leading to Theatre Alley and the other alleys and interior courtyards that honeycomb this Forbidden Town.

11. Loo Tai Cho Building, c. 1893

In 1890, Loo Gee Wing purchased E 40' of Lot 444 for $4,000 from William J. Macdonald and W 30' of Lot 443 for $3,000 from Henry F. Heisterman.[13] Three years later, Loo Tai Cho bought both pieces of the land on which this building was built (Fig. 58). He sold the property to the Musgrave family for $11,000 in February 1907.[14] Four years later, it was sold to Yee King Yum and Nip Lung Jim for $30,000.[15] In April 1974, Richard Pershing Joe purchased the property from Chow Kwong Hee for $11,000.[16]

This building, designed by William Ridgeway Wilson, is basically an Edwardian structure of three storeys, with a modest tin cornice defining the roofline. The ground floor is articulated with rustic columns and plaster detailing. Another interesting feature of the building is a rounded second-floor balcony above a splayed corner entry, marking the Fisgard Street entrance to Fan

Fig. 58. The Loo Tai Cho Building.

Tan Alley. Some windows on the second and third floors open to an iron balcony.

12. Yee King Yum Building, 1913

Yee King Yum and Nip Lung Jim bought a piece of land on W 30' of Lot 443 and E 40' of Lot 444, on which they built in 1913 a brick building behind Loo Tai Cho Building. This three-storey building, designed by Thomas Hooper, steps back slightly to allow more light into Fan Tan Alley. It is a plain structure, showing the rugged, utilitarian nature typical of Chinatown buildings fronting narrow passageways.[17]

13. Lee Woy's Fisgard Building, 1908

In August 1908, Lee Woy, Lee Yan, and Lee Chong purchased a piece of land on Lot 442 and E 30' of Lot 443 from the Todd Family for $36,000.[18] They had just enough money to build this small building on E 30' feet of Lot 443, leaving Lot 442 empty until 1910 (Fig. 59). Lee Woy's Fisgard Building has been in Chinese hands ever since. In October 1954, Dart Coon Club purchased this property from Lee Wa Kim and Edward Fook Lui Lum, selling it to Chee Kung Tong in February 1964 for $20,000.[19]

Fig. 59.
The Lee Woy's Fisgard Building.

The building was designed by Hooper and Watkins. Its original facade has been much altered, although the simple brick cornice and original iron balcony remain intact.

14. Hart's Fisgard Building, c. 1890

In July 1878, Michael Hart purchased Lot 455, on which a wooden hut once stood, from the Society of the Propagation of the Gospel in Foreign Parts, and leased the hut to the Chinese.[20] In March 1890 he bought Lot 464, facing Herald Street, from John H. Meldram.[21] In the same year he replaced the wooden huts with two brick buildings, one facing Fisgard Street, the other facing Herald Street (see the Hart's Herald Building in Chapter 13). Hart's Fisgard Building was again leased to the Chinese, who used the ground floor for a store and the second floor for tenements (Fig. 60). In November 1910, Michael Hart sold both lots (455 and 464) to Quan Yuen Yen and Joe Gar Chow, prominent Chinese merchants, for $35,000.[22] The properties remained in Chinese

Fig. 60. The Hart's Fisgard Building.

Fig. 61. The Quan Yuen Yen Building.

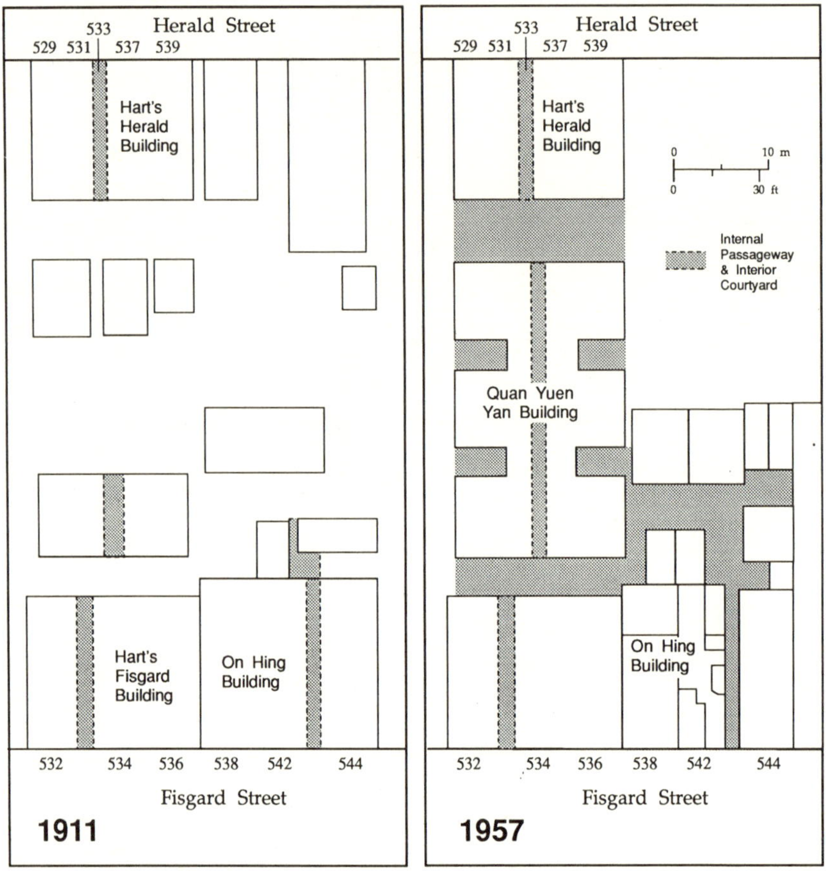

Fig. 62. The formation of internal passageways and courtyards at 532-544 Fisgard Street.

ownership until August 1945, when they were sold to A. Gillespie.[23] Frank Lee and Donald Lee, the current owners, bought the properties from the Western owner in 1979.

The Hart's Fisgard Building, now designated a heritage building, is a fine example of the Italianate style typical of early Chinatown building. Although its projecting wooden balcony has long been removed, the building still retains its finely detailed brickwork on the cornice and facade, and its evenly spaced segmental arched windows.

15. Quan Yuen Yen Building, 1912

This intermediate building, also a designated heritage building, was built partly on Lot 455 and partly on Lot 464, between the Hart's Fisgard and Herald buildings (Fig. 61). In 1912, Quan Yuen Yen and Joe Gar Chow commissioned Samuel Buttrey Birds, best known as the architect of Vancouver's Chalmers Presbyterian Church, to design this two-storey brick "lodging house."[24] It has an internal corridor on the ground floor and is accessible through the internal passageways of Hart's two buildings (Fig. 62). These three buildings, along with the On Hing Building, contain a series of internal passageways and interior courtyards, and are a showpiece of the evolution of the labyrinthine characteristic of Chinatown.

16. On Hing Building, c. 1891

The On Hing and Brothers Co., owned by Chan Tong Yu and Chan Tong Ork, was one of the largest import and export companies in Victoria's Chinatown. In 1882, the brothers bought the eastern and western halves of Lot 456 from James Porter and William H. Oliver respectively, for a total of $1,500.[25] The building was constructed circa 1891, its ground floor used for commercial concerns and the second floor for residents (Fig. 63). Fook Yuen Opium Factory operated in the rear during the 1880s and 1890s. After the death of the Chan brothers, the property was sold to C. Pelletier in November 1922, and held by Western owners throughout the 1920s and early 1930s.[26] In January 1935, Quan Yuen Yen and his wife purchased it for $4,000.[27] They used the ground floor for their herbalist store, Man Yuk Tong. Today, the building is owned by Frank Lee and Donald Lee, once the owners of Don Mee Restaurant.

In the early 1950s, Don Mee Choy Suey at 538 Fisgard Street was a small restaurant and butcher's store (Fig. 64) When the restaurant was expanded to the second floor in 1967, the On Hing Building was unsympathetically renovated: the elegant brick cornice was partially obscured by a modern eave and a false canopy; the segmental windows were modernized; and the facade of the ground floor was drastically altered.

17. Tong Ork On Hing Building, 1882 and 1914

In May 1882, the Chan brothers of On Hing & Brothers Co. purchased Lot 457 from Robert H. Austen for $1,250.[28] On the eastern half of the lot, they built a three-storey brick commercial

Fig. 63. The On Hing Building.

Fig. 64. The storefront at 538 Fisgard Street in the 1950s.

Fig. 65. The Tong Ork On Hing Building.

and residential building, using the lower floor as a cigar factory.[29] In October 1912, Chan Kai Bong, acting on behalf of the On Hing Co., borrowed $50,000 from the Dominion Trust Co. and used part of the loan to add another building on the western half of the lot (Fig. 65).[30] From June 1925, the property was owned by Lee Wa Kim.[31] It has remained in Chinese ownership, and is now owned by Henry Lee and Jack Lee; the latter is a former president of the Chinese Consolidated Benevolent Association.

This building has two parts: an eastern half, built in 1882, and a western half, built in 1914. When the western half was added, the decorative parapet of the eastern part was removed. The two buildings were then united by a common cornice treatment. The large, projecting, wooden balcony was removed and fire escapes added in 1955. The top floor has been left vacant since it was damaged by fire in 1965. The original facade of the building was much altered after the second floor was renovated for a restaurant and the ground floor for a grocery store.

18. CCBA Building, 1885

In March 1885, the Chinese Consolidated Benevolent Association (CCBA) purchased Lot 458 from Thomas D. Lindsay for $4,500, and built a three-storey brick building on the site (Fig. 66).[32] The

Fig. 66. The CCBA Building.

ground floor held stores, the second floor was used for the association's office, and the third floor housed the Palace of All Sages' and the Chinese Free School. Because of new fire and building codes, the upper floors were condemned and left vacant throughout the 1970s. In the early 1980s, the second and third floors were renovated, and are now being used as studios.

This Italianate building, designed by John Teague, is one of the most important and impressive commercial and institutional buildings in Chinatown. Its original facade displayed a double-tiered projecting balcony with wooden supporting posts, decorative corner brackets, fretwork and turned balusters, dividing screens, and decorative canopies. The Italianate cornice, window, and door heads of upper floors have been preserved, although the facade of the ground floor has been altered.

19. Lee's Association Building, 1911

In December 1909, Lee Mong Kow, Lee Dye (alias Lee Kum Jow), Lee Dan, and Lee Wing Yew, representatives of the Lee's Benevolent Association, purchased from the Chinese Empire Reform Association a piece of land on Subdivisions 13 and 14 of Lots 602 and 603.[33] Each subdivision measured only 20 feet by 120 feet. In 1911, the Lee's Association built two brick buildings

Fig. 67.
The Lee's Association Building.

which, described by a local reporter, "add[ed] greatly to the prominence of the thoroughfare" (Fig. 67).[34] Because of financial problems, the association kept the eastern building and sold the western building to Joseph H. Baker in October 1920.[35] In January 1935 the western building was purchased by the Shon Yee Benevolent Association.[36]

These two three-storey buildings, sharing a common party wall, have some similar features: both are faced with white glazed bricks and have eave-type cornices with a Chinese tiled roof and upturned corners. The higher eastern building, however, is more elaborate in decorative details. It contains a recessed balcony, with a tripartite arcade, and a "cheater floor." It also has a distinctive Beaux-Arts parapet and pediment panel. The most noticeable Chinese element of the lower western building is the horizontal sign of the Shon Yee Benevolent Association, written in large Chinese characters.

Fig. 68. The Gee Tuck Tong Building.

20. Gee Tuck Tong Building, 1903

Gee Tuck Tong (GTT) was formed by the Chinese surnamed Chow, Choy, Ng, and Yung or Cho, and the Yee Fung Toy Tong by people surnamed Yee. In June 1903, the two tongs pooled their money to buy Lot 605 from Leon Curtat, constructing a two-storey building on the land (Fig. 68).[37] GTT owned W 40' and Yee Fung Toy Tong E 20'. In December 1937 the City of Victoria took possession of GTT's property for tax arrears, selling it to Chan Dun's family for $3,510 in March 1944.[38] By August 1949, the Chan family had bought the Yee Fung Tong's side of the property for $3,500 and become the sole owner of the lot.[39]

This building, built in the Edwardian-Italianate style, is one of the best preserved Chinatown buildings. Its slightly asymmetrical facade is vertically divided into three bays by pilasters, and horizontally differentiated into two registers.[40] Each bay contains an arched recessed balcony, beneath which is a "cheater floor." A semi-circular ridge ornament, inscribed 1903, caps a prominent Italianate cornice. This feature, together with the rhythm of the arched bays, constitutes a strangely Moorish-like facade.

Fig. 69. The GTT Rooming House.

21. GTT Rooming House, 1913

Percy Fox and Berrill were engaged in 1913 to build this tenement building on the rear portion of the GTT property (Fig. 69)[41]. This three-storey brick building is accessible from a very narrow passageway through the GTT Building to a tiny courtyard. It was a dilapidated structure until it was completely renovated in 1991.

22. Chinese Public School, 1909

In January 1908, the Victoria School Board passed a ruling stating that permits to attend public school would be issued only to native-born Chinese children (see Appendix III). As a result, many children born in China were denied admission to public schools, and had to attend the Lequn Free School instead; hence, it became overcrowded. To solve this problem, the CCBA purchased Lot 606 from Lim Dat and built a school on the site (Fig. 70). The new school, known as the Imperial Chinese School, was officially opened on 7 August 1909.

This impressive two-storey building, designed by David C. Frame, is a pagoda-like structure, set forty feet back from the

Fig. 70.
The Chinese Public School.

street, with a wrought-iron railing in front. The building is an outstanding example of a combination of Chinese and Western decorative elements. The tile roofing, upturned eaves and roof corners, and ornate wooden balcony, together with Italianate cornices, Gothic trefoils, and Moorish windows, contribute to this effect.

« 12 » *Heritage Buildings on Government Street*

Government Street within the precinct of Chinatown consists of five heritage buildings. The 1600-block buildings – Island Amusement Building and Lee Woy's Government Building – are dissonant with the streetscape of Chinatown. The 1700 block consists of a unique old building and a grouping of three tong buildings. The five heritage buildings on Government Street in Chinatown are:

23. Island Amusement Building at 1600
24. Lee Woy's Government Building at 1618–1628
25. Tong Yue and Tong Ork Building at 1712–1714
26. Yen Wo Society Building at 1713
27. CERA Building at 1715–1717

23. Island Amusement Building, 1913

In April 1896, Mary Elizabeth Bell inherited Lot 441 from Alfred J. Langley.[1] The Island Amusement Company leased the land from her in 1913 and built this theatre structure (Fig. 71), known for a time as the Kinema Colour Theatre. In December 1935 Bell lost the property to the City of Victoria for tax arrears.[2] In March 1942, 7-Up (B.C.) Ltd. purchased the property from the

Fig. 71. The Island Amusement Building.

City for $8,500.[3] During the Second World War, the structure was used as a variety theatre and the Victoria Ballroom, among other things. It was later altered for Centre Gardens under the supervision of David C. Frame.[4] In the 1950s it was used for roller skating. In December 1965, the Victoria Old Age Pensioners' Association No. 1 purchased the property for $60,000, and has been using it as a bingo hall ever since.[5]

This brick building is a good example of Georgian Revival style. Its two street facades display subtle brick detailing, restrained classical cornice work, and understated arched windows. More features are matched by a fine "Wedgewood" interior.[6] Although the theatre building is not in harmony with the streetscape of Chinatown, it does relate visually to the McPherson Theatre across Government Street.

24. Lee Woy's Government Building, 1910

Lee Woy, Lee Yan, and Lee Cheong pooled their resources in 1910 to build this brick building on Lot 442, which housed a combination of stores, offices, and tenements (Fig. 72; also see Lee Woy's Fisgard Building in Chapter 11). In June 1942, Lum Young Chow and Lee Wa Kim bought the property for $17,000, selling it in October 1954 to the Dart Coon Club for $81,000.[7]

Fig. 72. The Lee Woy's Government Building.

This building, at the corner of Government and Fisgard streets, is essentially Edwardian, with Renaissance-inspired details and a splayed corner entrance. C. Elwood Watkins was the architect, and T.A. Brydon the brickwork contractor.[8] The two street facades are divided horizontally into two principal zones with a dominant cornice divided by pilasters, which dissolve into a band of brickwork beneath the cornice. Similar to the Kinema Colour Theatre, this building shows little concession to Oriental tastes. The building was much damaged by fire on 31 October 1977. The ground floor is now occupied by offices and stores, the second is used by Wong Sheung Kung-Fu Club, and the third is tenements. The upper facade is still quite intact, although the facade at the street level has been changed.

25. Tong Yue and Tong Ork Building, 1897

In April 1891, Chan Tong Yue and Chan Tong Ork of On Hing & Brothers Co. purchased Lot 459 from William J. Macdonald for $10,000.[9] The property has been possessed by Chinese owners ever since, and is now owned by Gong Far Joe and Richard Pershing Joe.[10]

This is the oldest Chinatown building on Government Street (Fig. 73). Its two-bay facade contains two shop fronts, and two

Fig. 73. The Tong Yue and Tong Ork Building.

narrow doors provide access to the tenements above. The building also contains a "cheater floor," which is lit by the high clerestory windows of the first floor. A brick string course defines the two bays below a handsome tin cornice.[11]

26. Yen Wo Society Building, 1912

In January 1877, Tsay Ching and Dong Bang, two Hakka natives, bought a narrow plot of land (Subdivision No. 7 of Lots 602 and 603, measuring twenty feet wide and eighty feet long) from James Porter for $375, and established Tam Kung Temple on the site.[12] After the Yen Wo Society was formed, it took possession of the property in October 1911.[13] In the following year the old temple was demolished and replaced by this three-storey building (Fig. 74). The ground floor is occupied by stores, the second floor by tenements, and the third by Tam Kung Temple.

The building, designed by L.W. Hargreaves, is essentially Edwardian Classical, with Renaissance pilasters and cornices. However, it is readily identified as a Chinatown building by a flagpole, an English inscription of the association's name above the cornice, a recessed balcony on the top floor, a bank of blind fretwork above the second-storey windows, and English and Chinese bilingual signs at the street level.

Fig. 74. The CERA and Yen Wo Society buildings (left to right).

27. CERA Building, 1905

Prominent Chinese merchants such as Lee Folk Gay and Chu Lai were members of the Chinese Empire Reform Association (CERA) in Victoria. In January 1905, Lee Folk Gay, on behalf of the CERA, purchased the property at Subdivisions 5 and 6 of Lots 618 and 619, and used the top floor of the building as CERA headquarters (see Fig. 74). The Quong Man Fung Opium Factory operated at the rear of the building in the early 1900s.

After the establishment of the Republic of China in 1912, the CERA became virtually defunct. It sold the northern half of the building on Subdivision 5 to Lung Kong Kung Shaw, a tong formed by clansmen surnamed Lau, Kwan, Cheung, and Chiu. The southern half of the building on Subdivision 6 was acquired in December 1936 by the City of Victoria for tax arrears, and was later purchased in June 1955 by the Loo Gim Sing family, the current owners.[14]

This building is unique for its twin facades featuring recessed balconies, delicate wrought-iron balusters, arched windows, and lion heads at the rooftop finials (see Fig. 43). The original facade of the ground floor has been much altered, and the southern part of the building has lost its decorative parapet.

« 13 » *Buildings on Herald and Store Streets*

Except for one, the heritage buildings on Herald and Store streets within the precinct of Chinatown are not in harmony with its streetscape.

(A) Herald Street

28. Hook Sin Tong Building at 658–664
29. Hart's Herald Building at 529–539

(B) Store Street

30. Scott & Peden Warehouse at 1601–1613
31. S & P Additional Warehouse at 1615
32. Lim Dat Building at 1619–1627

28. Hook Sin Tong Building, 1911

In August 1904, Lee Kum Jow, alias Lee Dye, on behalf of the Hook Sin Tong, purchased Lot 626 in Block L from Albert Ofner for $3,500.[1] In 1911, the association engaged C. Elwood Watkins to design this building, and the Parfitt Bros. to construct it (Fig. 75). Since then the property has been continuously owned by the

Fig. 75. The Hook Sin Tong Building.

association. The ground floor is now rented to stores, and the upper floors are the association's office and tenements.

This building is one of the best examples of Chinatown architecture. Its skyline is dominated by a flagpole, and a high parapet wall capped by pressed-tin finials. Two round granite columns divide the recessed balcony on the third floor into a triple opening, and support ornate brackets instead of a simple abacus; this was a common practice in Chinatown buildings. The delicate fretwork pattern of the balustrade, with a prominent diamond motif, is repeated in the range of windows below.[2] The bracketed cornice carries roof tiling in the form of an eave. Above the cornice is an English inscription of the association's name.

The building is known for its unusual oval dome, which measures twelve by fifteen feet and stands more than six feet high atop the third floor of the building. The dome consists of twenty panels of about five thousand pieces of stained glass, each having a tulip motif (Fig. 76). The dome was deteriorating from lack of maintenance until 1979, when the association received a $5,750 grant from the B.C. Heritage Trust and engaged John McMillan to repair it.[3]

Fig. 76. The stained-glass dome of Hook Sin Tong Building.

Fig. 77. The Hart's Herald Building.

Fig. 78. The Scott & Peden Warehouse.

29. Hart's Herald Building, c. 1890

This building originally housed a livery stable and a carriage repair shop, necessitating the two large carriage entrances (Fig. 77). After November 1910, the building passed into Chinese possession, and served a number of functions over the years, including housing one of Victoria's most notorious bordellos on the second floor. Rooms were partitioned by two connecting closets, through which people could go from one room to another (see Fig. 15).

This is a very unusual two-storey building in Chinatown, because of its curious asymmetry. The symmetry of the facade on the ground floor is marked by a central doorway, two carriage bays, two doorways, and two windows, but the symmetry is destroyed by an extra doorway on the eastern side. Furthermore, the placement of the second-floor window is illogical. The building, a designated heritage structure, is connected by a common internal passageway to two other designated buildings, the Quan Yuen Yen and the Hart's Fisgard buildings (see Fig. 62).

30. Scott & Peden Warehouse, 1913

In September 1912, John A. Scott and William Peden purchased

Fig. 79. The S & P Additional Warehouse.

Lot 154 in Block G from the Worthington family for $60,000.[4] They built this three-storey warehouse the following year (Fig. 78). A spur of the Esquimalt and Nanaimo Railway once ran directly into the warehouse for the loading and unloading of feed and grain.

The building was designed by M.S. Farwell. Its original plain utilitarian facade was much altered in 1987 when the building was converted from a warehouse to a residential and commercial building. The extensive remodelling, which included new windows, storefronts, entry, and architectural details, was designed by William Patterson.[5]

31. S & P Additional Warehouse, 1913

This commercial building, originally a simple two-storey structure, was built as an addition to the adjacent Scott & Peden Warehouse (Fig. 79).[6] It was one of the many warehouses in this area that at one time housed feed, hay, and grain businesses. This structure was subsequently converted to a commercial building with the addition of an extra floor and new cornice, windows, and storefront.

Fig. 80. The Lim Dat Building.

32. Lim Dat Building, 1898

In August 1898, Lim Dat and Wong Soon Lim purchased this building from Dennis R. Harris for $7,000.[7] They used the ground floor for stores and the upper floor for tenements (Fig. 80). In December 1909 they sold it to F.M. Rattenbury, architect of the Parliament Buildings and Empress Hotel, for $32,500.[8] The property was owned by Caucasians until December 1935, when it was lost to the City of Victoria through tax arrears.[9] The second floor had always been used as Chinese tenements; in October 1939, however, John R. Waters bought the building from the City of Victoria for $2,500 and converted it into a machine shop.[10]

This Romanesque building, designed by Thomas Hooper, has a sophisticated facade design which includes a complicated series of wide arched bays interspersed with banks of rectangular windows.[11] This new arched style was being introduced to Victoria at this time by other architects as well, including Samuel Maclure.

« 14 » A Heritage Stroll through Time and Memory

Many Chinatown buildings constructed in the nineteenth and early twentieth centuries are still cohesively grouped, and present a public face to the main streets. The private faces of the claustrophobic alleys and courtyards that once concealed warrens of tenements, opium factories, brothels, gambling dens, small restaurants, and stores, however, are still unseen by outsiders. This part of Chinatown, the Forbidden Town, remains something of an enigma, even to local residents who have lived in Victoria for many years. To explore and appreciate the mystery of historic Chinatown, one must see it on foot. This chapter suggests a route of about 1.2 miles (1.9 kilometres) to trace the history of Chinatown. Old and recent photographs are used to compare past and present streetscapes. This self-guided walking tour starts at Centennial Square, where City Hall is located, and ends in front of the Gate of Harmonious Interest, the symbolic entrance to historic Chinatown (Fig. 81). At a normal pace, the tour will take about an hour to complete.

Stop 1: Centennial Square

Standing near the fountain in the square, you are in the former

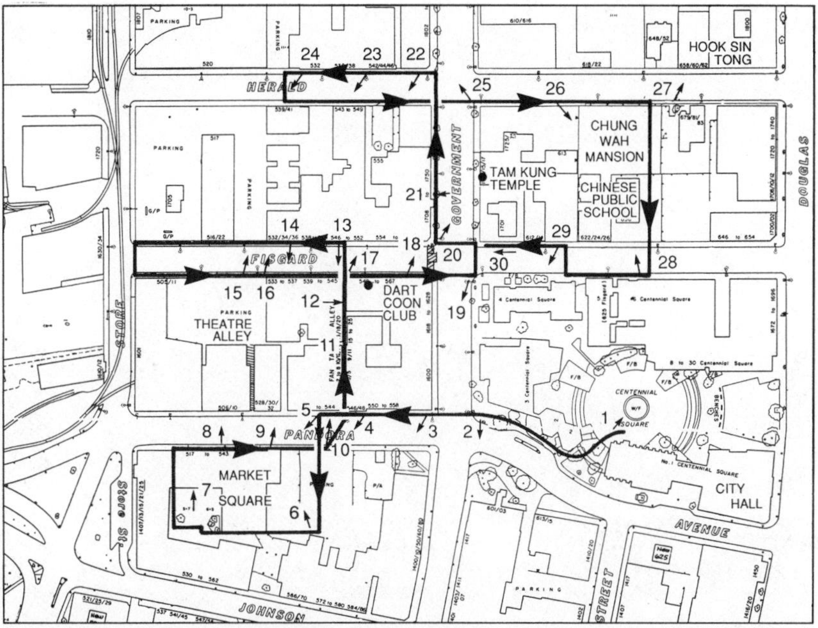

Fig. 81. The route of a walking tour of Chinatown.

Fig. 82. Central Fire Station, 626-634 Cormorant Street, in the 1910s.

Fig. 83. Chinese companies at 553-565 Cormorant Street in the 1900s.

600 block of Cormorant Street, the embryo of Victoria's Chinatown in 1858. During the Fraser River gold rushes, the Chinese owned half of the city block (see Fig. 1). The fountain is on the northern side of Cormorant Street, where the City Market, Central Fire Station, and Chinese tenement buildings were located. At one time, livestock and dairy produce were brought down from the Saanich Peninsula in the early morning and sold in the public market. The fire station and the buildings housing Wah Yun & Co. and Lee Dye & Co. were demolished in 1959 and 1960 when Centennial Square was developed as one of the City's centennial celebration projects in 1962 (Fig. 82). On the western side of the square is the former York Theatre, designed in the Italianate Renaissance style. It was rehabilitated as part of the Centennial Square project and renamed the McPherson Playhouse in 1965.

Stop 2: Pandora Avenue Realignment

Leave the square and walk towards Pandora Avenue on the southern side of Centennial Square, which was realigned in 1962 to the intersection of Government and Cormorant streets. Hence

Fig. 84. Headquarters of the Nationalist League at 533 Cormorant Street in the 1950s.

the 500 block of Cormorant Street between Government and Store streets became known as Pandora Avenue. It was the business centre of the budding Chinatown during the Fraser River gold rushes (see Fig. 4). In the late 1860s, for example, nearly half of the fifty Chinese business concerns were established here. At that time, Fisgard Street had less than five Chinese stores.

Stops 3 – 5: Southern Side of Pandora Avenue

At the corner of Government Street and Pandora Avenue was a series of brick buildings, which in the 1900s housed a few Chinese import and export companies such as Gim Lee Yuen, Hong On June, and Wong Man Sang (Fig. 83). The Kwong On Lung Opium Factory, operated from the early 1880s to 1908, was located behind them. All of these buildings have now been wiped out and replaced by a high-rise office complex which houses the Ministry of Forests.

Next to the Chinese import and export companies was a group of two-storey buildings, one of which housed the headquarters of the Chinese Nationalist League, or Kuomintang, in the

Fig. 85. Renovated buildings of Market Square shopping complex.

1950s (Fig. 84). These buildings have been demolished, and the site converted to an offstreet parking lot that slopes towards the bottom of the former Johnson Street ravine.

Further down Pandora Avenue is a group of beautifully detailed Italianate buildings which were constructed between the 1880s and the 1890s (Fig. 85). At one time they were rented to the Chinese, who used the ground floors for stores and the upper floors for living accommodation. In 1975, these brick buildings were restored and incorporated into the Market Square shopping complex.

Stop 6: Descending the Parking Lot

Walking across the street to the slanting parking lot, you will notice on your right the rear doors of buildings that once opened to the Johnson Street ravine (Fig. 86). Many old Chinese bottles and other artifacts were dug out when the site was being prepared for new development in the late 1980s.

Stop 7: Market Square

At the mini-amphitheatre inside Market Square, you are standing on the bottom of the former Johnson Street ravine. In the early 1890s,

Fig. 86. The facade of a building facing the former Johnson Street ravine.

Fig. 87. Wooden sheds facing the Johnson Street ravine in the 1890s.

Fig. 88. Street scene of Cormorant Street in 1880s.

you would have seen Chinatown's wooden huts perched on its steep bank (Fig. 87). The ravine seemed to be a "moat" separating the Forbidden Town from Victoria's city centre (see Fig. 2). In the late 1890s, the wooden structures were replaced by a series of two-storey tenement and retailing brick buildings (see Fig. 85).

Market Square is a quadrangle of nine connected buildings constructed between 1894 and 1900. Their backyards were once filled with wooden sheds, parked cars, and trash. Fort Victoria Properties purchased the buildings in 1974 and started to renovate them. The courtyard, designed by Nicholas Bawlf, features a two-storey balustraded gallery that encircles a landscaped amphitheatre.

Stop 8: Chinese Theatre and Theatre Alley

Leaving the mini-amphitheatre, walk up the former steep bank of the ravine and return to Pandora Avenue. Across the street you will see a parking lot that was the former site of the Chinese Theatre, once the focal point of Chinatown. The theatre was a simple brick structure with a large interior space. It was converted into a warehouse in the mid-1940s, then, after the 1960s, used as a market garden retailing store. The structure was demolished in the 1980s.

Fig. 89.
Pandora entry to Fan Tan Alley.

Although all traces of the theatre have been wiped out, Theatre Alley, the narrow passageway leading to it, is still partially intact; it is behind the closed door bearing the street number 526.

Stop 9: Northern Side of Pandora Avenue

The northern side of Pandora Avenue consists of a group of Italianate buildings that were typical of Chinatown development during the 1880s (Fig. 88). The picturesque Italianate style was popular in public and commercial buildings during the mid-nineteenth century because of its visual effect.[1] About six opium factories were established behind these buildings in the 1880s and 1890s. The broad wooden verandas extending from their fronts were removed in the late 1890s because of stringent fire regulations. The original facades have been changed, but some of the Italianate details are still intact, as shown by a current photograph of the same location. The Loo Chew Fan

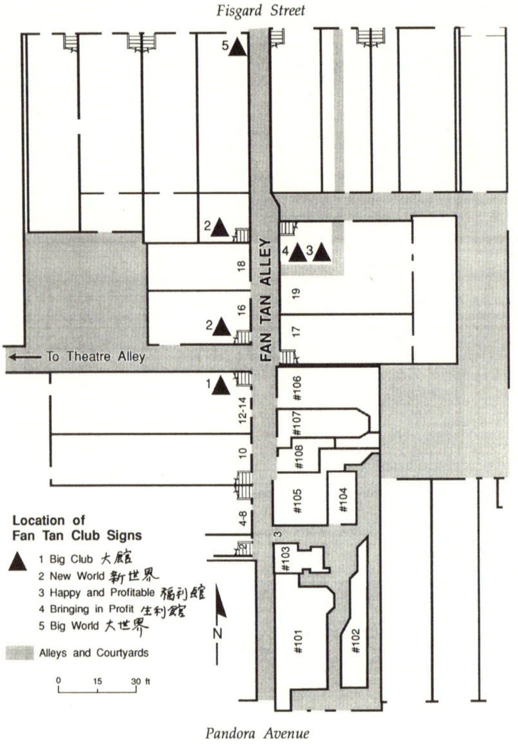

Fig. 90.
Fan Tan Alley and its exits.

Building now houses the headquarters of Hoy Sun Ning Yang Benevolent Association, the largest county association in Victoria.

Stops 10 – 12: Fan Tan Alley

Walking through Fan Tan Alley (see Chapter 5), you are now inside the mysterious section of the Forbidden Town (Fig. 89). The brick buildings lining this narrow pathway present a consistent streetscape that evokes the secretive nature of the Chinese community of the late nineteenth and early twentieth centuries. Chinatown is honeycombed with many century-old mid-block alleys, most of which are still closed off from public view (Fig. 90). Through these interconnected alleyways and courtyards, one could and still can go from Fan Tan Alley to Theatre Alley, Store Street, or Government Street.

Inside the alley, you can still see signs of Fan Tan clubs, written in Chinese characters. At one time, a heavy wooden door was installed near the Fisgard Street entrance to close the alley

Fig. 91. Decorations of Fan Tan Alley during the shooting of the movie Bird on a Wire.

off from strangers, and a peephole was used to screen visitors. You will notice this peephole on the brick wall to your right as you walk towards Fisgard Street.

Today, Fan Tan Alley is not only a functioning historic passageway, but also a location for such television and movie productions as *Stir Crazy* and *Bird on a Wire* (Fig. 91).

Stops 13 – 14: Southern Side of the 500 Block of Fisgard Street

The business centre of Chinatown gradually moved from Cormorant Street to Fisgard Street, which supplanted Cormorant as the core of Chinatown. In 1953, for example, about forty percent of the eighty Chinese business concerns in Chinatown were located on Fisgard Street; Cormorant Street had fewer than ten Chinese stores.

Although the streetscape of Fisgard Street has been much changed, some architectural features of its buildings remain. On both sides of Fan Tan Alley, you will see the higher Loo Tai Cho

Fig. 92. The Loo Tai Cho Building at 549-555 Fisgard Street in the 1920s.

Fig. 93. The Sheam and Lee Building at 539-545 Fisgard Street in the 1920s.

Fig. 94.
The Chinese Methodist Church at 526 Fisgard Street in the 1950s.

Building at 549-555 Fisgard Street on your left and the lower Sheam and Lee Building at 539-545 on your right (see Fig. 58). In the 1920s, the ground floor of the Loo Tai Cho Building housed four Chinese stores, Chung Lung Co., Hop Yick Co., Him Wo Tong, and Hong Get Co. (Fig. 92) Today its original arches have been changed to square openings, allowing the insertion of a "cheater floor." The Sheam and Lee Building housed Wo Yick Grocery, Shon Yuen Herbalist, and Wing Lee Yuen Dry Goods Store in the 1920s, and its storefront has also been altered (Fig. 93).

Further down the street you will see the Lee Chong Building at 533-537 Fisgard Street, where the Chinese Canadian Cultural Association is located. If the property owners allow you to enter the building alley, you can reach Pandora Avenue via a series of internal passageways and courtyards.

Stops 15 – 18: Northern Side of the 500 Block of Fisgard Street

Facing you is a parking lot that was the former site of the Chinese Methodist Church at 526 Fisgard Street (Fig. 94), officially opened on 13 March 1891.[2] Morning and evening services and Sunday school were conducted in the church until it was sold and demolished in 1962. Next to the parking lot is the Hart's Fisgard Building at 532-534; from here, you can reach Herald Street via a series of alleys and courtyards (see Fig. 62).

Next to the parking lot is the On Hing Building. Its original facade was much altered when Don Mee Restaurant opened on the second floor in 1967. Nevertheless, some of the building's features have remained; compare the 1900s photo (Fig. 95)

Fig. 95. The On Hing Building at 544 Fisgard Street in the 1900s.

showing the Ying Lung Store at 544 with the Tradewinds Gift Store at the same location. The large paper lanterns were hung out to celebrate the Chinese New Year festival. The two Chinese are standing in front of Yick Lung Co. at 544 Fisgard.

Further up the street are the Tong Ork On Hing and the Chinese Consolidated Benevolent Association buildings. In the 1880s, the wooden verandas in front of these buildings would have been striking (Fig. 96). These verandas were demolished in the late 1890s because of new fire regulations, and were replaced by projecting balconies supported by iron brackets.

At the corner of Fisgard and Government streets was a two-storey frame house (Fig. 97). The photograph, taken in the 1890s, shows a group of pupils lining up on the wooden sidewalk outside the association building. In October 1907, two rats infected with bubonic plague were caught in Seattle.[3] Fear of bubonic plague prompted Victoria City Council to carry out drastic improvements in Chinatown. Fifty pounds of arsenic-laced oatmeal were spread under all wooden sidewalks and around wooden structures throughout Chinatown. In the following two years, wooden sidewalks were replaced by concrete pavements, and many dilapidated wooden shacks and back verandas in Chinatown were demolished.

The frame house was torn down in 1939, and the site was left empty until Gar Nam Jong acquired the property and in 1946 built the present one-storey brick building.[4] The building, designed by D.C. Frame, has tiled roofs and other Chinese decorative components.

Fig. 96. A view of the Tong Ork On Hing and CCBA buildings in the 1880s.

*Fig. 97.
A street scene, corner of Fisgard and Government streets in the 1890s.*

Fig. 98. The Lee Woy's Government Building in the 1910s.

Stop 19: The 1600 Block of Government Street

The two massive buildings in the 1600 block of Government Street are not harmonious with the streetscape of Chinatown. In the 1910s, Pekin Chop Suey was located in the Lee Woy's Government Building (Fig. 98). Today the Wong Sheung Kung Fu Club is housed on the building's top floor. At one time, streetcars operated by the B.C. Electric Company ran along Government Street. The tracks were removed after the final streetcar run on 5 June 1948. The B.C. Electric Company, taken over by the provincial government in 1961, was then absorbed into what is now the B.C. Hydro and Power Authority.

Stops 20 - 21: The 1700 Block of Government Street

A group of brick buildings, at one time located on the northeastern corner of the intersection of Government and Fisgard streets, were owned by Mrs. Maude Dorothy Bishop (nee Worthington), one of the big Western landlords in Chinatown (Fig. 99). These buildings were demolished as Chinatown

Fig. 99. The 600 block of Fisgard Street in 1957.

continued to decline in the 1960s, and the demand for commercial and residential space decreased. The site is now occupied by a gas station. Next to it is a group of three association buildings. The ornate Tam Kung Temple was demolished in the early 1910s and is now housed on the third floor of the Yen Wo Society Building see Chapter 7). Next to this building was the former headquarters of the Chinese Empire Reform Association. An inscription of the association can still be barely seen beneath its parapet (see Chapter 6). The last tong building was the headquarters of Lung Kong Kung Shaw.

Stops 22 – 24: The 500 Block of Herald Street

Herald Street marks the northern boundary of Chinatown today. Opposite you is the Victoria Chinatown Care Facility, on the former site of the Chinese Hospital (see Appendix II). This facility provides intermediate care to about thirty elderly patients. The adjoining property at the corner of Herald and Government streets also belongs to the facility; an additional building for the same purpose will be constructed there. Next to the care facility is a typical Chinatown tenement building.

Further down the street is the Hart's Herald Building, a designated heritage structure that originally housed a livery stable

Fig. 100.
Tam Kung Temple and Empire Reform Association Building in the 1900s.

and a carriage repair shop. The second floor was once a brothel with rooms partitioned by two connecting closets (see Fig. 77).

Stop 25: The Lim Bang Building

This prominent three-storey building of tenements, offices, and stores at 1802–1814 Government Street is outside the Chinatown area today, but is historically significant to the Chinese community (Fig. 101). It was built in 1910 by a group of Chinese merchants and land speculators; two of them were Lim Bang and his brother, Lim Dat. Lim Bang was a very wealthy merchant and banker who owned a brickyard at Bazan Bay in North Saanich. Bricks from his plant were used for this building, and for the Douglas Hotel (opposite City Hall), which he also owned. The Lim Dat Building probably represents Chinese entrepreneurs' first

Fig. 101. The Lim Bang Building at 1804-1814 Government Street.

foray into this kind of investment in the 1910s. Unfortunately, the B.C. Land and Investment Co. foreclosed on their mortgages after the speculative land boom of the early 1910s failed. The building has never reverted to Chinese ownership.

This massive building runs the full length of the 1800 block of Government Street between Herald and Chatham streets. It is divided into three sections because of the sloping site, and features a series of massive arched bays and recessed balconies.

Stops 26 – 27: The 600 Block of Herald Street

Walking up Herald Street, you will see the Chung Wah Mansion (Fig. 102), built on the site of a former tennis court behind the Chinese Public School. The tennis court became a parking lot after the 1960s in order to generate income for the operation of the school. In 1986 the Chinese Consolidated Benevolent Association constructed the Mansion, a subsidized housing project funded by Central Mortgage and Housing Corporation.

Across the street is the Hook Sin Tong building, physically isolated from other similar buildings in Chinatown (see Fig. 75). This tong was formed by Zhongshan people. Some old-timers say that Dr. Sun Yat-sen, a Zhongshan native and the founder of the Republic of China, stayed there during his North American

Fig. 102. The Chung Wah Mansion, 655 Herald Street.

fund-raising tour in 1911. There is not a shred of evidence to support this assertion, however; it is just hearsay.

Stops 28 – 29: The 600 Block of Fisgard Street

A group of tong buildings is concentrated in this part of Chinatown. By far the most outstanding is the Chinese Public School, which houses the office of the Chinese Consolidated Benevolent Association (see Appendix III). Gee Tuck Tong no longer exists, but its tong building is one of the best examples of Chinatown structures. Its "cheater floor" is now used for storage.

Facing you are two tong buildings that housed the Shon Yee Association, the Victoria Chinese Cultural Centre Society, the Lee's Association, the Nationalist League, and Han Yuen. Walking across the street towards a parking lot, you will see what used to be the GTT Rooming House, another typical Chinatown tenement building. It was renovated and converted into an apartment building in 1991. Next to the police station is the location of the former Chinese Freemason Association. In February 1911 its members secured a bank loan of $12,000 using this building as security, and sent the money to China for the Huanghuagang Uprising against the Manchu Government.[5] The building was sold to the City and demolished in the early 1960s.

Fig. 103. The 500 block of Fisgard Street in the 1890s.

Fig. 104. The 500 block of Fisgard Street in 1988.

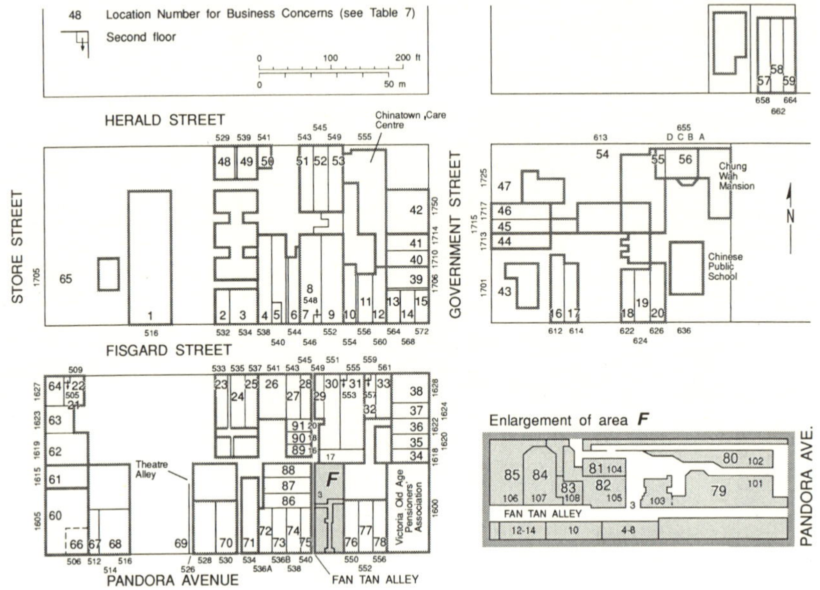

Fig. 105. Location of Business Concerns in Chinatown, September 1991.

The southern side of Fisgard Street now consists of a Senior Citizens' Activity Centre, a renovated police headquarters, a multi-storey parkade, and an arcade of specialty shops, which together form part of the Centennial Square precinct.

Stop 30: The Gate of Harmonious Interest

The gate is the focal point of Chinatown today (see Chapter 8). The two photographs show the view of Fisgard Street from the gate; one was taken in the 1890s (Fig. 103), the other in 1988 (Fig. 104). They show how much the streetscape of Fisgard has been altered in the past century.

At the end of this walking tour, you may be interested in shopping and dining in Chinatown. In September 1991 the types of businesses included restaurants, grocery stores, gift shops, galleries, and so on (Fig. 105 and Table 7, pg. 159).

Table 7
A List of Business Concerns in Chinatown, September 1991

Location Number	*Street Number*	*Name of Business Concern*
(A) Fisgard Street (north side)		
1	516	Songhees Imports International
2	532	Oriental Book and Gift Shop
3	534	Wah Yuen Grocery
4	538	Don Mee Restaurant
5	540	J. Tang Jewellers
6	544	Tradewinds Gift & Souvenirs
7	546	Hunan Village Restaurant
8	548	Wong's Restaurant.
9	552	Sun Hing Loung Grocery
10	554	Loy Sing Barbecue Store
11	556	Magpie Gift Studio
12	560	Wah Lai Yuen Restaurant
	562	Chinese Herb & Acupunture Centre (2nd fl.)
13	564	Foo Hong Restaurant
14	568	Ocean Garden Restaurant
15	572	Eastern Interiors Gift Shop
16	612	Forum Chinese Restaurant
17	614	Fung Hing Hong Herbalist Store
18	622	(Gladiolus Bakery
19	624	& Cafe in preparation)
20	626	Lin Heung Restaurant
		Victoria Star (2nd fl.)
(B) Fisgard Street (south side)		
21	505	Chow & Fleischauer Architects
		Arrow Mechanical Design
		Silver Image Studio
		Mohawk Data Services
22	509	Ocean Phoenix Restaurant
23	533	The Living End (second-hand clothes)
24	535	Chinese Canadian Friendship Association
25	537	Picture Framing
		Kindred Spirit (2nd floor)
26	541	Fan Tan Gallery
27	543	Kimbo Restaurant
28	545	Tiki Gallery
29	549	Fan Tan Cafe
30	551	Chinatown Trading Co.
31	555	Jan K Co.
32	559	Purple Boutique (in preparation)

33	561	Dynasty Jewellers

(C) Government Street (west side)

34	1618	Wong and Iverson
35	1620	Marwon Agencies Ltd.
		Wong Sheung Kung Fu Club (2nd fl.)
36	1622	The Victoria Travel Shoppe Ltd.
37	1624	South China Antiques and Art Crafts
38	1628	Quonley's
39	1706	Peking House Restaurant
40	1710	Choi Hung Books and Gifts
41	1714	Wai Fatt Chinaware & Grocery
42	1750	Capital City Auto

(D) Government Street (east side)

43	1701	Chevron Gas Station
44	1713	Mirari Inc.
45	1715	Metropolitan Diner
46	1717	Tai Sang Grocery
47	1725	Victoria Brake Specialty

(E) Herald Street (south side)

48	529	Vacant
49	539	Vacant
50	541	Vacant
51	543	Douglas Signs Ltd.
52	545	Prolific Screen Printing
53	549	Welcome Sales Co. Ltd.
54	613	Bunn Bros Automotive Service
55	655D	Merit Electronics
56	655A,B,C	Herald Street Artworld

(F) Herald Street (north side)

57	658	Vacant
58	662	Viberg Boot Mfg. Ltd.
59	664	Kata Trading

(G) Store Street (east side)

60	1605	Swans Pub Cafe
61	1615	Swans Gold Room
62	1619	Kaz Japanese Food
		Brass and Woodwind Shop
		North Park Gallery
		Angel Faul
63	1623	Matrix Marble Corporation
64	1627	Vacant
65	1705	Vacant

(H) Pandora Ave (north side)

66	506	Swan's Hotel
67	512	Vacant

68	514	Vacant
69	528	Vacant
70	530	Vacant
71	534	Munns Lumber Ltd.
72	536A	Storage
73	536B	Alley Antiques
74	538	Residence
75	540	Hoy Sun Benevolent Association
76	550	The Mustard Seed Street Church
77	552	The Mustard Seed Outreach
78	558	The Mustard Seed Food Bank

(I) Fan Tan Alley

79	3	#101 Hil's Cafe
80	3	#102 Designers Co-op
81	3	#104 Dragon-ware
82	3	#105 Polar Cow Imports
83	3	#108 Harlem Wig Shop
84	3	#107 The Turn Table
85	3	#106 Black Madonna
86	4–8	Vacant
87	10	Newtown Barber Stylist
88	12–14	Vacant
89	16	La Paz Raku Studio Gallery
90	18	Hearts Content
91	20	Howarth
92	17	Vacant

(J) Chinese Restaurants and Gift Shops close to Chinatown

721 Fisgard Street	Golden City Restaurant
1327 Government Street	Victoria Garden Restaurant
1411 Government Street	The Orient Gift Company
560 Johnson Street	Jade Palace Restaurant

Appendix I – The Origin of a Chinatown Myth

> *Animal rights activists are expressing outrage after October shoppers reported boxes of Manchurian miniature water buffalo horns for sale in Chinatown. Most biologists believe the Manchurian water buffalo to be extinct. . . . The discovery of hundreds of horns in the market place has caught the attention of natural history researcher Sandy Hull. . . . Hull plans to be in town Friday to launch a full-scale investigation into the sources of the horns and the slaughter of the Manchurian miniature water buffalo. . . .*
>
> *The Manchurian miniature water buffalo is described in detail in* Animal Curiosities of the Orient . . . *by Lady Jay Walken-Seymour, pub. 1881. Walken-Seymour tells of the Emperor Hi Lee Sung, who kept for 47 years in his private garden a little old buffalo he'd inherited from his grandmother, the dowager conservationist Ho Lee Kau. . . .*
>
> *Hull admits to being baffled about the source of horns found in Chinatown. His researchers have not ruled out the possibility that a Manchurian immigrant family with a tradition of planning ahead brought a few buffalo with them in the nineteenth century and have been breeding them in secret ever since.*[1]

Maureen O'Dea, a freelance writer, wrote this article and illustrated it with a photograph of the miniature horn in *The Victoria Star* in October 1988. Soon after it was published, I was besieged with telephone calls about the miniature buffalo horns in Chinatown. Most Chinese seeing the picture will readily recognize it is a photograph of *Ling Jiao*, the fruit of Ling (*Trapa bicornis*) (Fig. 106). Ling, a species of water chestnut, or Caltrops (*Trapa natans*), is an aquatic plant which bears numerous multi-branched roots and grows in shallow water and on muddy ground in China and other parts of Asia[2]. The plant has two kinds of leaves; the submerged

Fig. 106.
Leaves and fruit of water chestnut.

leaves have narrow, feathery blades, and the floating leaves are broadly diamond-shaped and usually mottled or variegated. Between June and August numerous white flowers grow in the axils of the leaves, which are above water. The dark-grey fruit, one to two inches across, is one-seeded and bears two "horns" as the botanical name, *Trapa bicornis*, suggests.[3] The white stone of Ling Jiao is tasty and nourishing, since it contains much protein, fat, and starch. In China it is usually eaten boiled, or ground into flour. Its use as food is often associated with the Cowherd and Spinster Festival on the 7th day of the 7th lunar month, and the Mid-Autumn Festival on the 15th day of the 8th lunar month. In 1988, the two festivals fell on 18 August and 25 September respectively; thus Maureen O'Dea saw Ling Jiao being sold in Chinatown.

I telephoned Miss O'Dea and asked her who Sandy Hull and Lady Jay Walken-Seymour were. She told me that she had invented the entire story; the persons she mentioned were all fictitious. She had no intention of discrediting Chinatown merchants. Her objective in writing this story was merely to "poke fun at people who believe everything written in the newspaper." I found her article amusing, but some people found it offensive. As Miss O'Dea predicted, some people always believe whatever nonsense the papers print. Sometime in the future, another writer may consult her article and repeat what she has written. If her tale, like other invented stories about Chinatown, were passed from one writer to another, it might eventually become another Chinatown myth. I do not wish to let this fraudulent report stand.

Appendix II – The Chinese Hospital

The Chinese Consolidated Benevolent Association (CCBA) began running a hospital, or *Taipingfang* (Peaceful Room), soon after its establishment in 1884.[1] For fifteen years the *Taipingfang* was run in a rented hut. In 1899, the CCBA constructed a two-storey brick building at 555 Herald Street and used it as *Zhonghua Yiyuan* (the Chinese Hospital). Without a regular income to support the free hospital, the association had to rely on donations. As a result, the hospital was always confronted with financial difficulties. By 1921, the hospital was twenty-two years old, and the building was badly in need of repair. Accordingly, the CCBA organized the first large-scale fund-raising campaign in April 1922, soliciting donations from all of the Chinese communities on Vancouver Island.[2] A total of $7,500 was raised. The renovation of the hospital building began in August and was completed two months later. A big celebration was held on 11 November 1922 to commemorate the renovation.

The CCBA had been exempted from paying tax on its hospital property since the hospital was operated. For reasons still unknown, the City began in the mid-1920s to impose municipal taxes on the hospital, aggravating its financial difficulties.[3] The City eventually took possession of the hospital property for $700 in tax arrears. Without money to redeem the property, the CCBA rented it from the City for $30 per month, and continued to operate the hospital. During the Great Depression of the 1930s, the CCBA was close to bankruptcy.

On 13 March 1938, it decided to close the hospital at the end of the month. Surprised by this decision, the City Council became most interested in seeing the CCBA maintain the hospital and look after its own people. As an inducement, the Council reduced the monthly rent to $20, and gave the hospital a monthly subsidy of $50 for the first four patients, and $10 for each additional patient.[4] The Chinese Hospital was then registered as a convalescent home, and placed under the jurisdiction of the City Medical Health Officer.

In November 1941, the Chinese Hospital was licensed as a private hospital rather than a convalescent home; Dr. Richard Felton, the City Medical Officer, became its first superintendent.[5] Two years later the Chinese Hospital was converted into the seventh first-aid post, which would serve as an auxiliary hospital for Chinese casualties during an emergency.[6] After the Second World War, the Chinese Hospital was licensed as a nursing home, and had twenty-two beds. Throughout the late 1940s and early 1950s, neither the City nor the CCBA was sure which of them should be responsible for the administration of the facility. It was called the Chinese Hospital, but it was licensed as a nursing home and operated like a boarding house for elderly Chinese males convalescing after stays in the Royal Jubilee Hospital. Eventually, in June 1953, the City requested that the CCBA should take over the hospital administration and pay a monthly rent of $60. In 1961 the Chinese Hospital was again licensed as a hospital, and continued to receive subsidies from the City. After renovation, the hospital still admitted only elderly male Chinese patients. The building had aged nearly forty years since the last renovation in 1922. The CCBA did not have the money to repair the dilapidated building and prevent further deterioration. Another renovation was not carried out until 1964, when Dong Gong (alias Dang Kang Shun), a former labourer, died in the Chinese Hospital and bequeathed all his life savings to the hospital.[7] The renovation cost was $30,000, of which more than eighty percent came from his bequest.

The term Chinese Hospital has always been a misnomer because it has never been properly run as a hospital. Although it was licensed as a hospital, it did not conform to the Standards for Licensed Private Hospitals under the new Hospital Act. Accordingly, on 31 May 1977, the administrator of the Chinese

Fig. 107. Victoria Chinatown Care Centre

Hospital applied for a community care facility licence, ending the institution's operation as a hospital in the following month. As the institution also did not meet the new regulations governing Community Care Facilities, it was not qualified to be licensed as a community care facility and receive funding from the Long Term Care Program. Eventually, in December 1977, the Chinese Hospital was registered as a private boarding home for the elderly. Without a government subsidy, it continued to run a deficit, and was finally closed on 3 June 1979.

Soon after the closure of the Chinese Hospital, I conducted a survey on the need among elderly Chinese for a long-term care facility in Chinatown. About half of the 277 respondents stated that they would like to move into a Chinatown care home if such a facility were available.[8] I also interviewed a few elderly Caucasian patients, some of whom indicated that they would consider moving to a Chinese care facility because they enjoyed Chinese cuisine. The idea of a Chinatown care facility project also received much support from the city, provincial, and federal governments. Accordingly, the Victoria Chinatown Care Society, chaired by Dr. David Y.S. Liang, was formed to carry out the project.[9] The City leased the former hospital site to the society for ninety-nine years at one dollar per year.[10] The Canada

Mortgage and Housing Corporation provided construction costs of about $1.5 million, and the Ministry of Health subsidized the operating expenses. On 25 February 1982 the Victoria Chinatown Care Centre, a thirty-bed intermediate care facility, was officially opened by James A. Nielsen, Minister of Health.[11] Unlike the previous Chinese Hospital, the centre admits both males and females, as well as patients of non-Chinese ethnic origins. In September 1991, the facility headed by Laura Meyer, has a staff of seventeen, and thirty-one patients of whom six are Caucasians.

Appendix III – The Chinese Public School

At a meeting in January 1899, the CCBA decided to operate a free school on the top floor of its building at 554-560 Fisgard for the Chinese children in Victoria (see Fig. 97). Within a few months, the association succeeded in raising $3,000 for the school, known as Lequn Yishu (Enjoying Company Free School).[1] It was officially opened on 1 July 1899, and attended by thirty-nine pupils. They were divided into two classes; senior students in Class A studied the *Four Books* and *Five Canons*, and junior pupils in Class B studied the *Trimetrical Classic*, the *Book of Family Names*, and other elementary classics. Other associations in the early 1900s also organized Chinese schools or classes. For example, the Chinese Empire Reform Association ran Aiguo Xuetang (Patriotic School), the Chinese Freemasons organized Qinge Xuexiao (Educating Youth School), the Yue Shan Society operated Yushan Xiaoxue (Yue Shan Primary School), and the Methodists and the Presbyterian Church ran English classes and Sunday Schools for Chinese children and adults. A few wealthy merchants employed English tutors to give English lessons to themselves and their children at home.

The demand for educational segregation was started in February 1901 by a few white parents at Rock Bay Elementary.[2] They complained to the school board that the fifteen Chinese children at school were unclean, untidy, depraved, and ill-mannered, and requested that they be put in a separate school because they had a demoralizing influence on the white children. Frank Eaton, the City's superintendent of education, conducted an investigation and found the accusation unfounded.[3] The school teachers did not find the Chinese children unclean, untidy, or vulgar. On the contrary, they praised them for their good behaviour and diligence. After the school trustees disregarded their petition, the white parents sought support from the powerful Trades and Labour Council. On 29 October 1902, the Labour Council called for a public meeting, at which the school trustees were put under fire for several hours and pressured to secure a remedy for the presence of Chinese children in public schools.[4] Eventually, in January 1903, the school board decided to place all the junior Chinese children of Victoria, of which there were only fifteen, in a separate classroom in Rock Bay Elementary, leaving the few senior Chinese children in other public schools to study with white children. Thus, the issue of segregation was temporarily solved.

At the beginning of August 1907, nineteen Chinese children who had just arrived from China applied for permits to attend school. George Jay, the school board chairman, felt that they did not understand English, and would therefore impede the progress of the whole class if placed in the same classroom with white children.[5] Accordingly, the school board ruled on 29 August 1907 that no Chinese children were to be admitted to public schools "until they could so understand the English language as to be amenable to the ordinary regulations and school discipline."[6] The CCBA, in turn, engaged Fred Peters, a reputed Victoria barrister, to bring a suit against the school board, but it was lost.[7] In January 1908, the school board ruled that permits to attend public schools would be issued only to native-born Chinese children.[8] Under this new ruling, many Chinese children were not qualified to attend public school, so the CCBA had to place all the China-born children in the Lequn Free School and immediately began planning a larger school building. Throughout the summer of 1908, the association campaigned among Chinese communities across Canada to raise funds for the construction of a school at 636 Fisgard Street (see Fig. 70). The new school, known as the Zhonghua Xuetang (the Chinese Imperial School), was officially opened on 7 August 1909 by Xu Bingzhen, Chinese Consul-General at San Francisco.[9] Unlike the Lequn Free School, the Chinese Imperial School had both English and Chinese classes, and concentrated on improving the English standard of Chinese children so that they could be admitted to public school.

After the fall of the Manchu government and the establishment of the Republic of China in 1912, the school was renamed Huaqiao Gongli Xuexiao (the Chinese Public School).

The school is still financially subsidized by the CCBA as the tuition fee is very low; only $20 per month. The school hours are four to six p.m., Monday through Friday. Boys and girls, mostly ranging in age from six to fifteen, attend the Chinese school to learn the Chinese language (Cantonese), history, literature, painting, dancing and folksongs. The school is open to anyone irrespective of age and ethnic origin as long as he or she is interested in learning Chinese language and culture. At one time, one Caucasian woman and four Caucasian children attended the school. In September 1991, the school, headed by Daniel Chan, has five teachers, and fifty-one students, including one Caucasian girl. In addition to the week-day school, Saturday school is run from nine a.m. to 2:30 p.m. during which period Cantonese and Chinese painting classes are offered.

Appendix IV – The Chinese Cemetery

Pioneer Square was formerly the Quadra Street Cemetery, which was the first cemetery in Victoria, used from 1858 to 1873[1] (Fig. 108). Its northeastern corner was set aside for the Chinese, becoming the first Chinese cemetery in Victoria.[2] When the Quadra Street Cemetery became overcrowded, the Ross Bay Cemetery was established, opening for burials in 1873.[3] The cemetery was divided into twenty-one blocks; Block L at the southwestern corner was specifically set apart for the burials of "Aborigines and Mongolians" (Fig. 109). The first Chinese interred there, on 18 March 1873, was listed as "Chinaman No. 1."[4] The ensuing interred Chinese were recorded in similarly derisive terms as "Chinaman No. 2," "Chinaman No. 3," and so on. In the early 1880s, the Chinese set up an altar in Block L, which in time became known as the "Chinese Cemetery." When Block L was fully occupied, Chinese graves spilled over to the adjoining Blocks N and K.

The Ross Bay Cemetery was built on a slope dipping gently westward. Blocks L, N, and K in the western section were

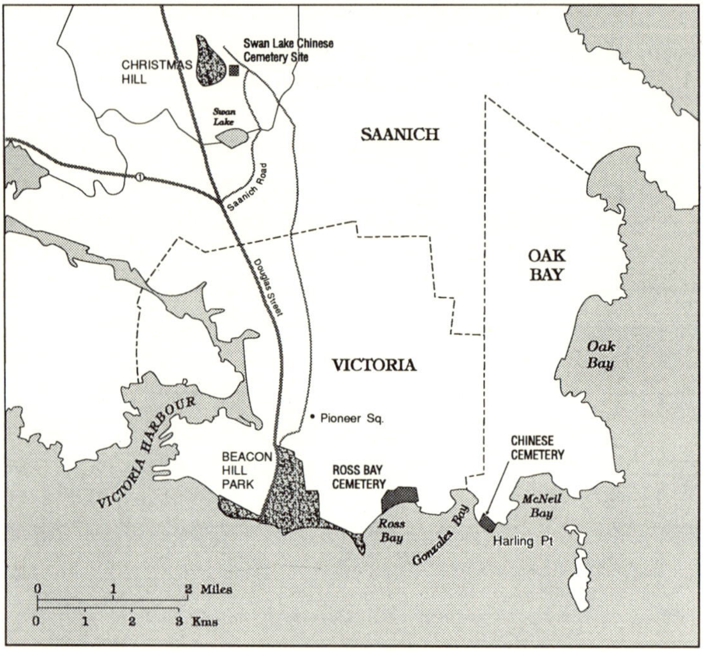

Fig. 108. Location of the Chinese Cemetery in Victoria.

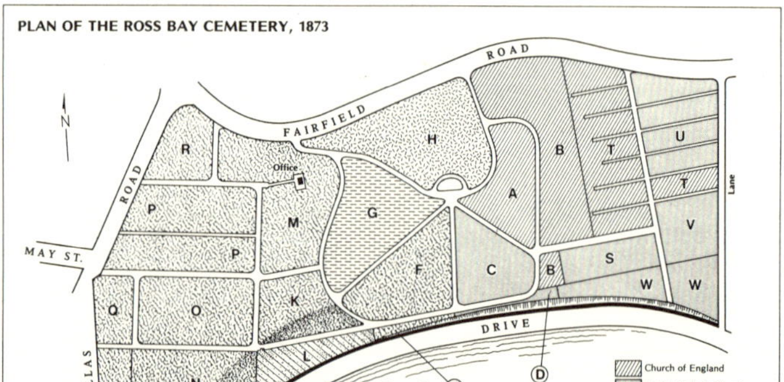

Fig. 109. Location of Chinese graves in the Ross Bay Cemetery.

low-lying, almost at sea level. They were usually flooded after heavy rainfalls, and lashed by high waves. Accordingly, the CCBA decided to establish its own cemetery, and probably engaged a geomancer to look for a good *Feng Shui* cemetery site – a site in harmony with Nature. Such a site was finally found in the Lake Hill Estate on the southern slope of Lake Hill (now called Christmas Hill), about half a mile north of Swan Lake.[5] On 30 October 1891, the CCBA bought a 8.75-acre lot from Alfred Williams for $2,200, intending to use it as a cemetery.[6] In those days, the Lake Hill Estate was still a wilderness where only a few farmers made their homes. But they were strongly opposed to having a Chinese cemetery on the estate. Earnest Geo. Hick, son of farmer George Hick, recalled, "One day along came some Chinese with a coffin and a body in a wagon for the burial. This piece of land joined our farm. Well, my father spotted what they were doing for they had already dug the grave. So he gathered up some neighbours, Jimmie and Joe Nicholson, Mr. Castleton, Mr. Kay, and Kenneth McKenzie, all armed with shotguns, and they drove the Chinamen off with their corpse."[7] Thus the cemetery site was left empty for more than ten years, as the Chinese were prevented from using it.

Over time, the "Chinese cemetery" at Ross Bay became so fully occupied that some graves had to be dug close to the marine drive. After several heavy storms, strong waves eroded a few waterfront graves, sweeping away the Chinese remains. In view of this situation, the CCBA sold the Swan Lake lot in 1902 and began looking for another good *Feng Shui* site.[8] It was soon found at Foul Point, at the end of a peninsula between Foul Bay (now known as Gonzales Bay) and Shoal Bay (now known as McNeill Bay) that was still a wilderness in the suburb of Victoria. In April 1903 the CCBA purchased a lot covering an area of 3.5 acres.[9] The Chinese Cemetery was immediately laid out and opened for burials; it was the first time the Chinese had their own cemetery. When the Municipality of Oak Bay was incorporated in 1906, the cemetery lay within its boundary; subsequently, the cemetery fell under the jurisdiction of Oak Bay instead of the City of Victoria. Foul Point then became popularly known as Chinese Point because of its cemetery. The point was officially renamed Harling Point by Oak Bay Council to commemorate the bravery of Dr. Fred Harling, a nearby resident who tried to rescue two persons from the waters off the Chinese Cemetery during a storm on 15 January 1934 and died from exposure.[10]

As Oak Bay developed, people began to settle in the neighbourhood of the Chinese Cemetery. Some of the nearby residents were much displeased with it. In September 1927 they lodged a complaint with Oak Bay Council, charging that the cemetery deterred urban development and prevented the construction of roads and general improvements in their neighbourhood.[11] Council also wanted to put the waterfront site of the Chinese Cemetery to other uses, but was advised by its solicitor that Council had no power to prohibit the Chinese from using the cemetery because the site had been a burial ground long before the municipality was incorporated.[12] Through the years, neighbours objected to the land being used as a cemetery. The Council of the 1930s tried legal action to close it, claiming that it was a threat to public health. However, Dr. Young, the Provincial Medical Health Officer, told Council that the cemetery was not a health hazard, that Council was, in fact, "unreasonably attempting to make unlawful something which had been lawful for a great many years."[13]

Burial plots in the Chinese Cemetery were not sold, but were "leased" for a term of six years. In the seventh year, the grave was opened, and the bones dug up, cleaned, and dried. They were then packed into a wooden crate, properly labelled, and stored in a brick house, known as the "bone house," in the cemetery. Thus the Chinese Cemetery was never fully occupied because the unearthed grave was used for another burial.

Crates of bones from Chinese communities across Canada were also sent to Victoria and stored in the bone house. They were sent back to China for reburial when the quantity was large enough to warrant a bulk shipment. Prior to 1909, each clan or county association organized its own shipment of bones. In order to reduce shipping costs, the CCBA decided to centralize the shipment, scheduling it once every seven years.[14] The Taishan Association was entrusted with the centralized shipment, and the first was carried out in 1909. The fourth shipment from the Chinese Cemetery to China took place in 1930. The fifth was scheduled in 1937, but was prevented by the outbreak of the Sino-Japanese War. All of the bones were stored in the bone house, awaiting delivery to China when the war was over. In the meantime, the CCBA stopped exhuming remains because the bone house was completely full. As a result, the available tomb sites were soon occupied. By the late 1940s, the cemetery was occupied by more than a thousand graves, and there was a rumour that some had been dug above others. The CCBA finally closed the cemetery in 1950. In the meantime, more and more people had begun to use the Royal Oak Burial Park.

After the People's Republic of China was established in 1949, shipping bones to China became impossible. From time to time mischievous children would break open the wooden door of the bone house in the Chinese Cemetery, take out the bones, and throw them at one another. The wooden door was replaced by an iron gate, but on one Halloween night rowdies threw firecrackers into the bone house, nearly causing a fire. A cement wall then replaced the iron gate and sealed up the bone house. In 1960, the CCBA succeeded in raising $18,000 for the reburial of hundreds of crates of bones.[15] The 820 unclaimed crates of bones were grouped according to home county and reburied in thirteen mass graves. The reburial ceremony on 15 October 1961 was probably the last elaborate Chinese funeral in the city.[16]

The Chinese Cemetery is in a deplorable condition, since it has not been in use for forty years. Many tombstones are badly weathered or broken. Some have been pulled out and scattered on the ground. Most of the vertical gravestones are tilted, and many tombs have caved in. A few tombs are still in good condition, but they are most vulnerable to vandalism. The cemetery, overgrown with grass, has become a stretch of wilderness. According to Dr. Adolf Ceska, Curator of Botany at the Royal British Columbia Museum, the Chinese Cemetery is a natural habitat for several endangered and rare wildflowers. The endangered group includes Macoun's Meadowfoam (*Limnanthes macounii trel*), Bear's Foot Sanicle (*Sanicula arctopoides*), and Greene's Rein-Orchid (*Piperia greenei*). The rare wildflowers include Few-flowered Shooting Star (*Dedecatheon pulchellum*), Broad-leaved Shooting Star (*Dodecatheon hendersonni*), Early Camas (*Camassia quamash*), White Fawn Lily (*Erythronium oregonum*), Chocolate Lily (*Fritllaria Lanceolata*), and Western Buttercup (*Ranunculus oregonum*).

With Dr. Ceska's help, I tried to identify some of these wildflowers in the cemetery. Shooting Star resembles cascades of shooting stars. Its blossom has reflexed magenta petals and a central beak-like stamen tube, composed of coloured anthers joined around the style[17]. The five-pointed calyx-lobes are usually flecked with purple, with a ring of clear yellow at the base of each lobe. The Early Camas, a loose cluster of wheel-shaped flowers punctuated with yellow anthers, usually tower above the grass-like leaves. The Camas, belonging to the Lily family, is one of the food plants used by Western Indians. Its root is a smooth onion-like bulb, plump and nutritious, forming as close a substitute for bread as anything that was available to primitive cooks.[18] The Western Buttercup is a common species from Alaska to California, although it is limited to the far *West*, as its name suggests.[19] In March, the Western Buttercup occurs in tremendous numbers near the shore of the Chinese Cemetery. At a distance it looks like a yellow carpet. Macoun's Meadowfoam is one of the rarest plants in the world, so much so that as recently as 1965 it was thought by U.S. researchers Howard Scott Gentry and R.W. Miller to be extinct.[20] It was first found in the Chinese cemetery in 1972, and from 1972 to 1980, more than thirty distinct populations of Macoun's Meadowfoam were sighted on Yellow Point north of Ladysmith and at a few other locations on southeastern Vancouver Island.[21] Today the Chinese Cemetery harbours one of the fifty-five populations of Macoun's Meadowfoam; this population is among the eight that have more than two hundred plants.[22]

Carpeted with a great variety of wildflowers in the spring and early summer, the Chinese Cemetery has attracted many naturalists. It is one of the rare natural wildernesses on Vancouver Island. Therefore, any beautification project for the Chinese cemetery should consider the preservation of its natural beauty.

Notes

Abbreviations

AFB Absolute Fees Book
CCBA Chinese Consolidated Benevolent Association
CV Heritage Conservation Branch, Research Division. *Chinatown Victoria*, August 1977.
DHI Foundation Group Designs Ltd. *Downtown Heritage Inventory*. City of Victoria, 1989.
DHMP Foundation Group Designs Ltd. *Downtown Heritage Management Plan*. City of Victoria, 1989.
LRO Land Registry Office, Ministry of Attorney-General, Province of British Columbia.
TOT City of Victoria, Heritage Advisory Committee. *This Old Town: Central Area Heritage Conservation* Report. City of Victoria, Revised Edition, December 1983.
VSB Victoria School Board.

Chapter 1

1 *Daily Globe*, San Francisco, 15 May 1858.
2 *The Victoria Gazette*, City of Victoria, 30 June 1858.
3 *The Colonist*, City of Victoria, 4 October 1932.
4 David Chuenyan Lai, *Chinatowns: Towns Within Cities in Canada* (Vancouver: University of British Columbia Press, 1988), pp. 4–8.
5 *Census of Canada*, 1880–81.
6 Canada. *Royal Commission on Chinese Immigration: Report and Evidence* (Ottawa: Printed by the Order of the Commission 1885), p. 398.
7 Canada. Statutes of Canada, An Act Respecting Chinese Immigration, 1923, Ottawa, 13–14 George V, Chap. 38, pp. 301–315.
8 Canada. Statutes of Canada. An Act to Amend the Immigration Act and to Repeal the Chinese Immigration Act, 1947. Ottawa, 11 George VI, Chap. 19, pp. 107–109.
9 Chuen-yan David Lai, "Socio-Economic Structures and Viability of Chinatown," in *Residential and Neighbourhood Studies in Victoria*, ed. C.N. Forward, Western Geographical Series, (Victoria: University of Victoria, Department of Geography, 1973), p. 120.
10 David Chuenyan Lai, *Chinatowns: Towns Within Cities in Canada*

(Vancouver: University of British Columbia Press, 1988), pp. 253-263.

[11]Betty Campbell, ed. *Royal Visit to Victoria, British Columbia, Canada*. Victoria: Campbell's Publishing Co. Ltd., 1983.

[12]*Chinese Times*, 6 February and 27 February 1986; *Chinatown News*, 18 January 1986, p. 22.

[13]*Chinatown News*, 3 March 1989, p. 26. Dr. Lam was sworn in on 9 September 1988 as British Columbia's twenty-fifth Lieutenant-Governor.

Chapter 2

[1]Harry Gregson, *A History of Victoria, 1842-1970* (Victoria: Victoria Observer, 1970), pp. 123-24.

[2]*The Victoria Gazette*, Victoria. 14 July 1858, p. 3.

[3]The size of a standard lot in Victoria was 60 feet wide and 120 feet long.

[4]British Columbia. Land Registry Office in Victoria. AFB, Vol. 2 Fol. 619, No. 14877.

[5]LRO. AFB Vol. 1 Fol. 213, No. 189.

[6]LRO. Cert. No. 14877-3

[7]LRO. Cert. No. 14877-14 and 14877-15.

[8]LRO. AFB Vol. 5 Fol. 776, No.2371. DD5323, and AFB Vol. 5 Fol. 845 #7492 DD 29063.

[9]C.Y. Lai, "Socio-economic Structures and Viability of Chinatown" in C.N. Forward (ed.), *Residential and Neighbourhood Studies in Victoria*, Western Geographical Series, Vol. 5, Chap. 3, pp. 101-129.

[10]LRO. AFB Vol. 9 Fol. 845. #7492 DD29063.

[11]"Chamber Reports on Oriental Situation Here," the *Victoria Daily Times*, 28 November 1921.

[12]If a property owner failed to pay the city tax, his or her property would be sold by the city's tax collector at a public auction known as Tax Sale. The owner was given one year's time to redeem his or her property from a Tax Sale. If the owner could not redeem his or her property at the end of a year's period, he or she would lose his or her property to the Tax Sale purchaser. If there was no buyer at a Tax Sale, the city would acquire the property.

[13]Ibid., Certificate No. 37065, No. 117710, and No. 123377.

Chapter 3

[1]*The Victoria Gazette*, 30 July 1858.

[2]*The Victoria Gazette*, 15 March 1859.

[3]*The Victoria Gazette*, 22 October 1859.

[4]*British Colonists*, 1 January 1866.

[5]Morton, James, *In the Sea of Sterile Mountains*, Vancouver: J.J. Douglas Ltd., 1974, p. 9.

[6]Chuen-yan David Lai, "Chinese Imprints in British Columbia," *BC Studies*, No. 39, Autumn, 1978, p. 28.
[7]David Chuenyan Lai, "The Chinese Cemetery in Victoria," *BC Studies*, No. 75, Autumn, 1987, p. 24.
[8]J.E. Spencer, "Chinese Place Names and the Appreciation of Geographic Realities," *Geographical Review*, Vol. 31, 1914, pp. 79–94.
[9]"New Spelling for Names and Places," *China Reconstruct*, No. 3, 1979, p. 45.
[10]John Joe, private interview, October 1989
[11]A fictitious name is used here because the interviewee does not want to be identified.
[12]David Chuenyan Lai, "Impacts of Canadian Immigration Policies on Chinese Migration, 1858-1988," *Asian Culture*, Vol. 14, April 1990, p. 181.
13Bessie Tang, private interview, November 1990. Her brother, Liu Guang Zu, was known to the host society as Joseph Hope, and her other brother, Liu Guang Ying, as Ying Hope, formerly an alderman of the City of Toronto.
[14]*Henderson's Greater Victoria City Directory and Vancouver Island Gazetteer*, "Chinese, Japanese, and Hindoo Business Firms, 1912," Victoria: Henderson Publishing Co., 1912.
[15]*Wrigley's B.C. Directory*, Victoria: Wrigley's Publishing Co., 1919, p. 1079 and p. 1093.
[16]Mrs. Wong Wu Kiu, private interview, November 1990.
[17]*The Colonist*, 9 August 1878.
[18]*The Colonist*, 29 August 1922.
[19]A fictitious name is used here because the interviewee does not want to be identified.
[20]David Chuenyan Lai, *Chinatowns: Towns Within Cities in Canada*. Vancouver: University of British Columbia Press, 1988, pp. 190–191.

Chapter 4

[1]"The Chinatown in British Columbia," *Chambers's Journal*, 10 June 1911 pp. 440–441.
[2]Charles Goldie, engineer of underground services, City of Victoria, interview held in June 1982 and Nov. 1988. Mr. Goldie was aware of the underground water cistern before the excavation.
[3]N. de Bertrand Lugrin, "Victoria Chinatown Mysteries 50 Years Ago," *Victoria Sunday Times Magazine*, 25 August 1951, p. 3.
[4]*The Colonist*, 7 January 1930.
[5]*The Colonist*, 9 May 1885.
[6]Chuen-yan Lai, "The Chinese Consolidated Benevolent Association in Victoria: Its Origins and Functions," *BC Studies*, No. 15, Autumn, 1972, p. 65.

Chapter 5

[1]"The Chinese in British Columbia," *Chambers's Journal*, 10 June 1911, p. 441.

[2]LRO. AFB Vol. 6 823 #3485a. DD7812.

[3]LRO. AFB Vol. 6 Fol. 486 #3062a, and Vol. 7 Fol. 305 #3949a.

[4]Canada, House of Commons, Sessional Papers, 1907–8, Paper No. 10, pp. 52–53.

[5]Canada, Statutes of Canada, 7–8 Edward VII, Chap. 50, An Act to prohibit the importation, manufacture and sale of opium for other than medicinal purposes, 20 July 1908.

[6]Ibid., 24 January 1916.

[7]*Wrigley's British Columbia Directory*. Vancouver: Wrigley Directories Ltd., 1923, p. 1613.

[8]A Chinese elderly man who did not wish to be identified, private interview, October 1981.

[9]"Fan Tan Alley," *Real Estate Victoria*, Vol. 5, No. 14, April 9–15, 1981, p. 1.

10"New Old Town Shapes Up," *Victoria Business Review*, November 1983, p. 5.

[11]*Greater Victoria B.C. City Directory, 1987*. "Street Directory of Householders and Businesses" (Vancouver: B.C. Directories Ltd., 1987), p. 140.

Chapter 6

[1]*Victoria Times*, 19 March 1970.

[2]Clark, Cecil, "A True Police Adventure," *Daily Colonist* Magazine Section, 6 September 1959, p. 8.

[3]Lum Fook Wing, President of the Shon Yee Association, Victoria interview, October 1989; and A Special Issue on the 70th Anniversary of the Establishment of the Shon Yee Association in Vancouver, 1914–1984. Vancouver: the Shon Yee Association of Canada (no date of publication), p. 14.

[4]Freedman, M., Chinese Lineage and Society: Fukien and Kwangtung, London: the Athlone Press, 1966, p. 167.

[5]Chuen-yan David Lai, "Contribution of the Zhigongtang in Canada to the Huanghuagang Uprising in Canton, 1911," *Canadian Ethnic Studies*, XIV, 3, 1982, p. 98.

[6]Cameron, M.E., *The Reform Movement in China, 1891–1912,* New York: Octagon Books, 1963.

[7]Lai, Chuen-yan David, "Contribution of the Zhigongtang in Canada to the Huanghuagan Uprising in Canton, 1911" *Canadian Ethnic Studies*, Vol. XIV, No. 3, 1982, p. 98.

[8]*The Colonist*, 31 Oct. and 13 Dec. 1916.

[9]Lee, David T.H., *A History of Chinese in Canada*. Victoria: Canada Liberty Publisher, 1967, p. 252 (in Chinese script).

[10]Chuen-yan Lai, "The Chinese Consolidated Benevolent Association in Victoria," *BC Studies*, No. 15, Autumn, 1972, p. 56.
[11]*Webster's Ninth New Collegiate Dictionary*. Springfield, Mass.: Merriam-Webster Inc., 1983, p. 1242.

Chapter 7

[1]N. de Bertrand Lugrin, "Victoria Chinatown Mysteries 50 Years Ago," *Victoria Sunday Times Magazine*, 25 August 1951, p. 3.
[2]Eric Cumine, *Hong Kong Ways and Byways* Hong Kong: Belongers' Publications Ltd., 1981, p. 110.
[3]Ngai Mau Sou, the temple keeper; Lee Tung Hoi, secretary of the Chinese Consolidated Benevolent Association, and some other Chinese oldtimers, personal interviews, in the 1970s.
[4]*The Colonist*, Victoria. 23 January 1876.
[5]British Columbia, Land Registry Office. AFB, Vol. 5, Fol.324, No. 182A- 20581. The legal description of the lot is Subdivision Lot 7 of Lots 602 and 603, City Block M.
[6]Ibid., On 14 October 1911 Tsay Ching and Dong Sang sold the property to Yen Wo Society at $1.00.
[7]"Artifacts Lost in Temple Fire," *Victoria Times* 12 January 1980, and "Fire Loss Saddens Chinese" *the Sunday Colonist*, 13 January 1980.
[8]Letter, from Gordon Hanson, M.L.A., to R. Sing, President of Yen Wo Society, 25 January 1980.
[9]Dan Bensky and Andrew Gamble (Compiled and translated). *Chinese Herbal Medicine Materia Medica*. Seattle: Eastland Press, 1986, p. 290.
[10]Xie, Zhufan, and Huang Xiaokia, ed. *Dictionary of Traditional Chinese Medicine*. Hong Kong: the Commercial Press Ltd., 1984, pp. 157–158.
[11]Mr. Wong Pong Cheung, formerly a Chinese doctor in Hong Kong, Victoria, interview, March 1991.
[12]Mr. Ng Yuk Lun, Senior Temple Overseer, caretakers of temples, and local residents, personal interviews in January 1991.
[13]James Zee-Min Lee, *Chinese Potpourri* Hong Kong: the Oriental Publishers, Third Edition, 1961, p. 162.
[14]Jonathan Chamberlain, *Chinese Gods,* Hong Kong: Long Island Publishers, 1983, pp. 105–106.
[15] Ibid., p. 107.
[16]The statuette of Confucius was lost when the shrine was moved from the old CCBA Association building to the Chinese Public School. The large statuette of Confucius on the altar table was donated to the Association by the Taiwan Government.
[17]"Chinese Shrine Rites Sunday," *Colonist*, 21 May 1966 and "Shrine Honors Chinese Pioneers," *Times*, 24 May 1966.
[18]Zheng Chuanyin and Zhang Jian, ed. *Zhongguo Minsu Cidian* (Chinese Myths Dictionary) Hong Kong: Shangwu Publishing Co., 1987, p. 456.

[19]*Ci Hai Dictionary* Taiwan: Chung Hua Book Company, 1979, Vol. III, p. 4215 (in Chinese script).
[20]*Ci Hai Dictionary* Taiwan: Chung Hua Book Company, 1979, Vol. III, p. 3761 (in Chinese script).
[21]*Ci Hai Dictionary* Taiwan: Chung Hua Book Company, 1979, Vol. III, p. 4610 (in Chinese script).
[22]Yuan Ke, ed. *Zhongguo Shenhua Chuanshuo Cidian* (A Dictionary of Chinese Myths As They Are Told). Hong Kong: Shangwu Publishing Co., 1982, p. 65.

Chapter 8

[1]David Chuenyan Lai, *Chinatowns: Towns Within Cities in Canada*, Vancouver: University of British Columbia Press, 1988, pp. 261-262.
[2]Zhiping Liu, Chinese Architecture (Beijing: Architecture Publishing Co., 1957), pp. 64-65 (in Chinese script).
[3]D. Mitra, *Buddhist Monuments*. Calcutta: Sahitva Samad, 1971, p. 21. The torana at the northern quadrant consisted of two pillars with capital supporting a superstructure of three curviform architraves.
[4]Patricia Bahree, "A Graveyard Celebrates Life." *Orientations*, June 1979, p. 42.
[5]*Chinatown News*, 18 Feb. 1988, p. 18.
[6]Chuen-yan David Lai, *Arches in British Columbia*, Victoria: Sono Nis Press, 1982, pp. 22-23.
[7]City of Victoria. Chinatown Ad Hoc Committee. *A Plan for the Rehabilitation of Chinatown*, 1979, p. 4.
[8]The construction cost does not include the city crew's labour which was valued at about $59,000.
[9]C.A.S. Williams, *Outlines of Chinese Symbolism and Art Motives*. Tokyo: Charles E. Tuttle Co., 1978, p. 367.
[10] Ibid., p. 421.
[11]China's five major ethnic groups are the Hans, Manchus, Mongolians, Muslims, and Tibetans. The Five Powers in Dr. Sun's proposed constitution are executive, legislative, judicial, examination and supervision powers.
[12]Lou Qingxi, "All Kinds of Lion," *China Reconstruct*, February 1986, p. 33.
13Chuen-yan David Lai, *The Gate of Harmonious Interest: From Concept to Reality*, Victoria, City of Victoria, 1982, 2nd Printing, p. 7.

Chapter 9

[1]Alastair W. Kerr, "The Architecture of Victoria's Chinatown," *Datum*, Vol. 4 No. 1 Summer, 1979, pp. 8-11.
[2]Genevieve B. Wimsatt, "Romances of the Roofs," *Art and Archaeology*, Vol. 27 April 1929, p. 178.

[3]J. H. Edgar, "The Origin of the Chinese Roof: A Theory," *Journal W.C. Border Research Society*, Vol. 5 1932, p. 130.
[4]Else Glahn, "Chinese Building Standards in the 12th Century," *Scientific American*, Vol. 244, May 1981, p. 162
[5]Warren E. Cox, *The Romance of Chinese Art*. New York: Garden City Publishing Co., 1960, p. 27.
[6]C.A.S. Williams, *Outlines of Chinese Symbolism and Art Motives*, Tokyo: Charles E Tuttle Co., 1978, pp. 323-324.
[7]Ibid., p. 414.

Chapter 10

[1]LRO. AFB Vol. 20 Fol. 260 #7012, DD 5977.
[2]LRO. 67706-I.
[3]LRO. B40567.
[4]DHI. p. 218.
[5]DHI. p. 120.
[6]LRO. 7752-I.
[7]LRO. 89402-I DF 27836 and DF23837.
[8]LRO. 131974-I.
[9]LRO. 358019-I DF 87824 and DF98318.
[10]CV. 3. Lum Sam Building, c. 1884 (Primary), pages unfolioed.
[11]LRO. 103208-I DF 36669.
[12]LRO. 125944-I.
[13]LRO. 255510-I.
[14]LRO. AFB Vol. 6 Fol. 486 #3062a, and Vol. 7 Fol. 305 #3949a.
[15]LRO. AFB Vol. 9 Fol. 727 #7487a, and AFB Vol. 22. Fol. 143 # 10459a and #10640a.
[16]DHI. 2-6 Fan Tan Alley, p. 75.
[17]CV. Lim Bang Building, c. 1885 (Primary), pages unfolioed.
[18]LRO. AFB Vol. 6 Fol. 823 #3485a. DD7812.
[19]LRO. 37065-I, and 117710-I DF 44151.
[20]LRO. 123377-I.

Chapter 11

[1]LRO. AFB Vol. 20 Fol. 114 #6960c.
[2]LRO. 95858-I DF 31837.
[3]LRO. 121327-I and 161687-I.
[4]LRO. 238872-I.
[5]TOT. 535 Fisgard Street c. 1900.
[6]CV. Lee Building, 1901 (Primary), pages unfolioed.
[7]LRO. AFB Vol. 6 Fol. 765 #3410 DD 15766F, and Vol. 7 Fol. 21#3552a DD 15766-F.
[8]LRO. AFB Vol. 9 Fol. 877 #7508a DD 15766-F; DHI, p. 79.
[9]LRO. AFB Vol. 11 Fol. 653 #10389a DD15766-F.
[10] LRO. AFB Vol. 35 Fol. 80 #15766F DF3787.

[11]LR). 201017-I.
[12]DHI. 8-14 Fan Tan Alley, p. 76.
[13]LRO. AFB Vol.12 Fol. 79 3 #10634a and Fol. 225 #11202a, DD 7142.
[14]LRO. IFB Vol.1 Fol. 159 #486-I DD 7142.
[15]LRO. IFB Vol. 3. Fol. 175 #2677-I DD 24411.
[16]LRO. C53907.
[17]DHI. 15-23 Fan Tan Alley, p. 76.
[18]LRO. 2757-I 998-I DD11235.
[19]LRO. 257339-I and 350157-I.
[20]LRO. AFB Vol. 5 Fol. 782 #2334.
[21]LRO. AFB Vol. 11. Fol. 479 #9981.
[22]LRO. AFB Vol. 28 Fol. 255 #25294.
[23]LRO. 155643-I.
[24]DHI. p. 28.
[25]LRO. 51058-I.
[26]LRO. 51058-I.
[27]LRO. 95919-I.
[28]LRO. AFB Vol. 7 Fol. 253 #3870a.
[29]DHI. p. 80.
[30]LRO. AFB Vol. 33 Fol. 451 #8596-I DD 8596-F.
[31]LRO. 60400-I.
[32]LRO. IFB Vol. 1 Fol 28 #99-I and AFB Vol. 8. Fol. 895 #6291a, DD 987.
[33]LRO. AFB Vol. 28 Fol. 310 #23502c DD 17303.
[34]"New Buildings for Fisgard Street," *Victoria Daily Colonist*, 22 September 1910.
[35]LRO. 47976-I.
[36]LRO. 96819-I.
[37]LRO. AFB Vol. 21 Fol. 235 #8828c, and 83407-I.
[38]LRO. 112607-I DF39599, and 142860-I.
[39]LRO. 197881-I
[40]CV. Gee Tuck Tong Benevolent Association Buildings, 1903, pages unfolioed.
[41]DHI. p. 87.

Chapter 12

[1]LRO. AFB Vol. 24 Fol. 82 #14480 82410-I DV 3224.
[2]LRO. 103208-I DF 36670.
[3]LRO. 150932-I.
[4]Geoffrey Castle, "Hall Recalls Chinese Pioneers and Early Architect," *Times Colonist*, 22 April 1989.
[5]LRO. 374363-I.
[6]CV. "Theatre/Bingo Hall," pages unfolioed.
[7]LRO. 131758-I and 257339-I.
[8]TOT. p. 56.
[9]LRO. AFB Vol. 1 Fol. 30 #104-I DD 1093.
[10]LRO. 40549-W DF 113040 and 40550-W DF 113046.

[11]CV. Yue, Tong, Ork Building, pages unfolioed.
[12]LRO. AFB Vol. 5 Fol. 324 #1861A DD 20581.
[13]LRO. AFB Vol. 29 Fol. 436 #2625F DD20581.
[14]LRO. 107793-I, and DF 81495 283647-I.

Chapter 13

[1]LRO. AFB Vol. 22 Fol. 104 #10305, DD 28349, and F99718 AFB Vol. 22 Fol. 120 #10372.
[2]CV. Hook Sin Tong Association Building, 1911. Pages unfolioed.
[3]"A Painstaking Puzzle in Repairing Glass Dome," *Victoria Times*, 26 July 1979.
[4]LRO. AFB Vol. 31. Fol. 310 #7144f. DD27085.
[5]DHI. Scott & Peden Warehouse, p. 220.
[6]DHI. Scott & Peden Warehouse, p. 221.
[7]LRO. AFB Vol. 9 Fol. 151 #4803a. DD10474.
[8]LRO. AFB Vol. 27 Fol. 285 #23054. DD10474.
[9]LRO. 103208-I.
[10]LRO. 116692-I.
[11]CV. 1601 Store Street, pages unfolioed.

Chapter 14

[1]Alan Gowans, *An Architectural History of Canadian Life*. Toronto: Oxford University Press, 1966, p. 104.
[2]The Colonist, 15 March 1891.
[3]The Victoria Times, 29 October 1927.
[4]LRO. 148656-I, and 148655-I. On 6 December 1944 the southern 80 ft. of Lot 459 was owned by Gar Nam Jong, and the northern 40 ft of Lot 459 by Joe Dick Kee. The brick building was built on the southern section of the lot, and Tong Yue and Tong Ork Building, a much older building, was built on the northern section (see Chapter 12). In January 1962 George Joe owned both sections of the lot and willed them to Gong Far Joe and Richard Pershing Joe after his death in 1968.
[5]David Chuenyan Lai, "Contribution of the Zhigongtang in Canada to the Huanghuagang Uprising in Canton, 1911, "*Canadian Ethnic Studies*, XIV, 3 1982, pp. 95-104.

Appendix I

[1]Maureen O'Dea, "Tiny Buffalo Dehorned for Fast Buck? Conservationists Fear Slaughter," *The Victoria Star*, 19-25, 1988, p. 5.
[2]Helen L. Pursey, ed. *The Hamlyn Encyclopedia of Plants*, London: The Hamlyn Publishing Groups Ltd., 1975, p. 16.

[3]S.G. Harrison, G.B. Masefield, and Michael Wallis, *The Oxford Book of Food Plants*, Oxford: Oxford University Press, 1969, p. 32.

Appendix II

[1]For details of the history of the Chinese Hospital in Victoria, see David Chuenyan Lai, "From Self-segregation to Integration: The Vicissitudes of Victoria's Chinese Hospital," *BC Studies* No. 80, Winter, 1988-89, pp. 52-68.

[2]CCBA Annual Report, 1922. Minutes of meeting on 13 January, and on 9, 17 and 25 April, 1922.

[3]A letter from City Treasurer to T.M. Miller, a lawyer for the CCBA, dated 15 December 1921.

[4]Minutes of the Municipal Council of Victoria, 4 and 11 April, 1938; and *Letter Book of the City of Victoria*, 4 January – 30 December, 1938, 4032.

[5]Ibid., 3 November 1941, and Letter Book of the City of Victoria, 15 December 1941, 3127.

[6]*Victoria Times*, 10 June 1943.

[7]Court Registry, Law Courts, Victoria. *Dong Gong's Will*.

[8]Lai, Chuen-yan David, *A Care Home in Victoria's Chinatown*: A Survey of the Need. Victoria: Capital Regional Hospital and Health Planning Commission, 1979, p. 1.

[9]"Victorians Set to Dedicate Chinatown Home Care Facility." *Chinatown News*, 3 February 1982, p. 15.

[10]Letter, from Mark Johnston, Administrative Assistant, City of Victoria, to Chinese Consolidated Benevolent Association, 18 October 1979.

[11]*Times-Colonist* 17 February 1982.

Appendix III

[1]CCBA Annual Report, 1899, Minutes of meeting, 8 January 1899.

[2]For details of the educational segregation issue, see David Chuenyan Lai, "The Issue of Discrimination in Education in Victoria, 1901-1923," *Canadian Ethnic Studies*, XIX, 3, 1987 pp. 47-67.

[3]*The Colonist*, 13 November 1902.

[4]*The Colonist*, 30 October 1902.

[5]*The Colonist*, 24 August 1907

[6]VSB. *Minutes 1905–1910*, Meeting on 29 August 1907, p. 77.

[7]Ibid., Meeting on 11 September 1907, p.78.

[8]Ibid., Meeting on 8 January 1908, p. 89.

[9]*Times*, 6 and 7 August 1909; *Colonist*, 7 August 1909.

Appendix IV

[1]For details of the history of the Chinese Cemetery, see David

Chuenyan Lai, "The Chinese Cemetery in Victoria," *BC Studies*, No. 75, Autumn, 1987, pp. 24–42.

[2]G. French, "The Burial Places of Early Victoria (Part 3)." a xeroxed copy of a newspaper clipping kept by J. Adams. (Name of newspaper and date of publication unknown).

[3]J. Adams, *Historic Guide to Ross Bay Cemetery* Victoria: Heritage Architectural Guides, 1983, pp. 4–5.

[4]Burial Records, Ross Bay Cemetery, Victoria.

[5]Chuen-yan David Lai, "A Feng Shui Model as A Location Index," *Annals of the Association of American Geographers*, 64, 1974, pp. 506–513.

[6]LRO. Conveyance from Alfred William to the CCBA, 30 Oct. 1891. *Register of Absolute Fees*, Vol. 9 pp. 165–66. No. 5405a, and Vol. 13, p. 144, No. 13036a.

[7]Letter, from Earnest Geo Hick of 3871 Saanich Road, Victoria, to Mr. Helmcken. Victoria City Archives: Ethnic Group, Chinese: G.I. 012.001.

[8]LRO. Conveyance, CCBA to George Hick, 4 June 1902, D.D. Pocket 25482.

[9]LRO. Conveyance, Mary Williams to the CCBA, 3 April 1903, D.D. Pocket 987.

[10]*Victoria Times*, 16 January 1934.

[11]*Oak Bay Municipality Correspondence*, No. 3501, a letter from Councillor Crease to CCBA, 6 November 1927.

[12]Ibid., no. 3501, letters from Bodwell and Lawson to Oak Bay Council, 16 September and 7 October 1927

[13]Ibid., no. 7600. a letter from Bodwell and Lawson to Council, 23 May 1933.

[14]CCBA Annual Report, 1908. Minutes of meeting on 22 May 1908.

[15]CCBA Annual Report, 1960. Minutes of meeting on 12 May 1960; CCBA Annual Report, 1961. Minutes of meeting on 1 March 1961.

[16]*Victoria Times*, 16 October 1961, and *Victoria Colonist*, 17 October 1961.

[17]Tim Fitzharris, *Wildflowers of Canada* Toronto: Oxford University Press, 1986, p. 38.

[18]Leslie L. Haskin, *Wild Flowers of the Pacific Coast* Portland: Metropolitan Press, 1934, p. 30.

[19]Lewis J. Clark, *Wild Flowers of British Columbia* Sidney, British Columbia: Gray's Publishing Ltd., 1973, p. 161.

[20]T. Pawlick, "Meadowforma Microcosm," *Harrowsmith* (October 1980): 43.

[21]Adolf and Oldriska Ceska, "Status Report on Limnanthes macounii Trel (Limnanthaceae), April 1987" (Unpublished manuscript), p. 2.

[22]Personal interview with Dr. Adolf Ceska, 17 April 1989.

Bibliography

Adams, J. *Historic Guide to Ross Bay Cemetery* Victoria: Heritage Architectural Guides, 1983.

Bahree, Patricia. "A Graveyard Celebrates Life." *Orientations*, June 1979, pp. 41–44.

British Columbia. Heritage Conservation Branch, Research Division. *Chinatown Victoria*, August 1977.

British Columbia. Land Registry Office, *Absolute Fees Book*. British Columbia Directory. Victoria, 1882–1932.

Cameron, M.E. *The Reform Movement in China, 1891–1912*. New York: Octagon Books, 1963.

Campbell, Betty, ed. *Royal Visit to Victoria, British Columbia, Canada*. Victoria: Campbell's Publishing Co. Ltd., 1983.

Canada. *Royal Commission on Chinese Immigration: Report and Evidence* (Ottawa: Printed by the Order of the Commission, 1885).

Canada. Statutes of Canada, An Act Respecting Chinese Immigration, 1923, Ottawa, 13–14 George V, Chap. 38 pp. 301–315.

Canada. Statutes of Canada. An Act to Amend the Immigration Act and to Repeal the Chinese Immigration Act, 1947. Ottawa: 11 George VI, Chap. 19, pp. 107–109.

CCBA Annual Reports. Archives of the Chinese Consolidated Benevolent Association of Victoria.

Ceska, Adolf and Odriska. "Status Report on Limnanthes macounii Trel (Limnanthaceae), April 1987" (unpublished manuscript).

Chamberlain, Jonathan. *Chinese Gods* Hong Kong: Long Island Publishers, pp. 198.

Ci Hai Dictionary Taiwan: Chung Hua Book Company, 1979. (in Chinese script)

City of Victoria. Heritage Advisory Committee. *Downtown Heritage Inventory*. Prepared by Foundation Group Designs Ltd., 1989.

City of Victoria. Heritage Advisory Committee. *This Old Town: Central Area Heritage Conservation Report*. Revised Edition, December 1983.

City of Victoria. Minutes of the Municipal Council of Victoria.

City of Victoria. Letter Book of the City of Victoria.

City of Victoria. Minutes of Victoria School Board, 1905-1910.

Cumine, Eric, *Hong Kong Ways and Byways* Hong Kong: Belongers' Publications Ltd., 1981.

Clark, Lewis J. *Wild Flowers of British Columbia*. Sidney, British Columbia: Gray's Publishing Ltd., 1973.

Edgar, J.H. "The Origin of the Chinese Roof: A Theory," *Journal W.C. Border Research Society*, Vol. 5 1932, pp. 130–132.

Fitzharris, Tim. *Wildflowers of Canada*. Toronto: Oxford University Press, 1986.

Glahn, Else. "Chinese Building Standards in the 12th Century," *Scientific American*, Vol. 244, May 1981, pp. 162–173.

Gowan, Alan. *An Architectural History of Canadian Life*. Toronto: Oxford University Press, 1966.

Gregson, Harry. *A History of Victoria, 1842–1970* Victoria: Victoria Observer, 1970.

Harrison, S.G., G.B. Masefield, and Michael Wallis, *The Oxford Book of Food Plants*, Oxford: Oxford University Press, 1969.

Haskin, Leslie L. *Wild Flowers of the Pacific Coast*. Portland: Metropolitan Press, 1934.

Kerr, Alastair W. "The Architecture of Victoria's Chinatown," *Datum*, Vol. 4 No. 1 Summer, 1979, pp. 8–11.

Lai, Chuen-yan. "The Chinese Consolidated Benevolent Association in Victoria: Its Origins and Functions," *BC Studies*, No. 15, Autumn, 1972, pp.53-67.

Lai, Chuen-yan David. "Socio-Economic Structures and Viability of Chinatown," in *Residential and Neighbourhood Studies in Victoria*, ed. C.N. Forward, Western Geographical Series, (Victoria: University of Victoria, Department of Geography, 1973), pp. 101–129.

—. "A Feng Shui Model as a Location Index," *Annals of the Association of American Geographers*, Vol. 64, 1974, pp. 506–513.

—. "Chinese Imprints in British Columbia," *BC Studies*, No.39, Autumn, 1978, pp.20-29.

——. *A Care Home in Victoria's Chinatown: A Survey of the Need*. Victoria: Capital Regional Hospital and Health Planning Commission, Victoria, 1979.

———. "Contribution of the Zhigongtang in Canada to the Huanghuagan Uprising in Canton, 1911" *Canadian Ethnic Studies*, Vol. XIV, No. 3, 1982, pp. 95–104.

—. *The Gate of Harmonious Interest: From Concept to Reality*. Victoria, City of Victoria, 1982, 2nd Printing.

———. *Arches in British Columbia*, Victoria: Sono Nis Press, 1982.

Lai, David Chuenyan. "The Chinese Cemetery in Victoria," *BC Studies*, No. 75, Autumn, 1987, pp. 24–42.

——. "From Self-segregation to Integration: The Vicissitudes of Victoria's Chinese Hospital," *BC Studies*, No. 80, Winter, 1988–89, pp. 52–68.

——. "The Issue of Discrimination in Education in Victoria, 1901–1923," *Canadian Ethnic Studies*, XIX, 3, 1987, pp. 47–67.
——. *Chinatowns: Towns Within Cities in Canada* Vancouver: University of British Columbia Press, 1988.
——. "Impacts of Canadian Immigration Policies on Chinese Migration, 1858–1988," *Asian Culture*, Vol. 14, April 1990, p. 181.
Lee, David. T. H. *A History of Chinese in Canada*. Victoria: Canada Liberty Publisher, 1967 (in Chinese script).
Lee, James Zee-Min. *Chinese Potpourri*. Hong Kong: the Oriental Publishers, Third Edition, 1961.
Liu, Zhiping. *Chinese Architecture* Beijing: Architecture Publishing Co., 1957 (in Chinese script).
Lou Qingxi. "All Kinds of Lion," *China Reconstructs*, February 1986, pp. 32–34.
Mitra, D. *Buddhist Monuments*. Calcutta: Sahitva Samad, 1971.
Morton, James. *In the Sea of Sterile Mountains*, Vancouver: J.J. Douglas Ltd., 1974.
Oak Bay Council. *Oak Bay Municipality Correspondence*.
O'Dea, Maureen. "Tiny Buffalo Dehorned for Fast Buck? Conservationists Fear Slaughter," *The Victoria Star*, 19–25, 1988, p. 5.
Pawlick, T. "Meadowforma Microcosm," *Harrowsmith*, October, 1980.
Pursey, Helen L. ed. *The Hamlyn Encyclopedia of Plants*. London: The Hamlyn Publishing Groups Ltd., 1975.
Ross Bay Cemtery. *Burial Records*.
Shon Yee Association of Canada. *A Special Issue on the 70th Anniversary of the Establishment of the Shon Yee Association in Vancouver*, 1914–1984. Vancouver: the Shon Yee Association of Canada (no date of publication).
Spencer, J.E. "Chinese Place Names and the Appreciation of Geographic Realities," *Geographical Review*, Vol. 31, 1914, pp. 79–94.
Warren E. Cox. *The Romance of Chinese Art*. New York; Garden City Publishing Co., 1960.
Williams, C.A.S. *Outlines of Chinese Symbolism and Art Motives*. Tokyo: Charles E. Tuttle Co., 1978.
Wimsatt, Genevieve B. "Romances of the Roofs," *Art and Archaeology* Vol. 27 April 1929, pp. 175–185.
Xie, Zhufan, and Huang Xiaokia, ed. *Dictionary of Traditional Chinese Medicine*. Hong Kong: the Commercial Press Ltd., 1984.
Yuan Ke, ed. *Zhongguo Shenhua Chuanshuo Cidian* (*A Dictionary of Chinese Myths As They Are Told*). Hong Kong: Shangwu Publishing Co., 1982.
Zheng, Chuanyin and Jian Zhang, ed. *Zhongguo Minsu Cidian* (*Chinese Myths Dictionary*) Hong Kong: Shangwu Publishing Co. 1987 (in Chinese text).

Index

Index

__David Chuenyan Lai__ is a professor of geography at the University of Victoria. He has been the chairman of the Chinatown Redevelopment Committee since 1979, chairman of the Saanich Heritage and Archival Advisory Committee for two years, and member of the Heritage Advisory Committee of the City of Victoria for ten years. In 1980 he was named as an Honorary Citizen of the City of Victoria in recognition of his work in Victoria's Chinatown, and in 1983 he was appointed as a Member of the Order of Canada (C.M.) in recognition of his distinguished service in the Chinese community. His efforts in heritage conservation, and the preservation of Victoria's Chinatown have been recognized by a broad range of awards, citations, and honours, including the Association of American Geographers' Applied Geography Citation Award, the American Association of State and Local History Award of Merit, the Heritage Canada Foundation Regional Community Service Award, the Heritage Society of British Columbia Annual Award, and the Hallmark Society Award of Merit.